PRAISE

"If you've ever felt like you needed to "be" a certain way to fit the expectations of others, this book is must-read. It will feed your soul in unexpected ways! Eileen inspires us with her courage to explore that there is "MORE" to life. I had tears, laughter, and so many "aha" moments while reading this book. It brought me a deep sense of healing and connection."

Karen Hammond, M.A. Counseling

"Through her deep introspection and observation of the world around her, Eileen passionately narrates the path of awakening available to all of us. She tells the intimate story of her own unfolding with tenderness and ferocity that can inspire us and teach us to face our own journeys courageously."

Jeff Ellias-Frankel, Ph.D. Psychologist

"Eileen Marder-Mirman has written a thoughtful memoir that reflects upon the experiences in her life that led her to pursue spiritual healing. Her willingness to be open and honest with herself encourages her readers to be equally brave in identifying the pieces of their lives that don't feel quite right. It helps others determine how they, too, can find a path to more peace within and move towards healing."

Lila Edelkind, M.A. Education

"This book is a journey! From the intriguing stories of Eileen's family lineage to her struggles with inner conflicts and doubts... all so relatable and engaging, I couldn't put the book down.

The many questions she poses are so relevant that if we have even a small inkling to explore more than the superficial layers of our personality, this book can be the guide. She walks us intimately through her challenge allowing us to witness as she faces ALL parts of herself - no matter how contrary to the image of how she prefers. It brought up many of my own questions and conflicts in such a natural way that revelations came along the way with no pressure."

Karen Atkins, Singer-Songwriter, Vitality Educator

"This gem of a book is a deep and honest description of one woman's spiritual journey in the midst of a "regular" life. It offers readers both courage and hope, demonstrating how staying true to one's inner knowing can provide a path to the place we most yearn to reach—the healing and wholeness that awaits in our own hearts and souls."

Jane Sloven, Writer, Psychotherapist, Healer

"Eileen takes you on a magical journey painted so beautifully with her words. She shares a lifetime of wisdom, experience, and heartache both poignant and passionate. Magnificently laid before you like an elaborate feast to nourish your soul and expand your heart."

Donna Velasco, Transformational Life Coach

HOW I THINK
I SHOULD BE
IS B***S***!

FROM HIDDENNESS TO OPEN-HEARTED

HEALING MEMOIR
(NOT JUST) FOR PROFESSIONAL WOMEN

EILEEN MARDER-MIRMAN

DEDICATION

*For my husband, Jamie, who is finally
awakening from the bullshit.*

*For my son, Josh, who inspires me with his dedication
to living the best life possible with his loving wife,
Rebecca, and their son, Levi.*

And to Levi, the joy of my life, who opens my heart every day.

Without their abiding love this book would not exist.

TABLE OF CONTENTS

FOREWORD

When a teacher looks into the heart of a student, he or she sometimes sees the unique quality that student will bring to the world, often years later, when the student becomes a master healer themselves. The teacher senses the flavor of the teachings that is embodied in the student's being and how they will present not only "the way" to their own students, but *their way.*

What I know about Eileen Marder-Mirman is that she is determined, forthright, and never backs down from following her heart. Because of that, she is the passionate advocate of the heart of each person who comes to her for healing.

This book reveals Eileen's blueprint for her life. Each uncovering of her early suffering hides within it the plan she formulated throughout her life of how to move closer to the light. She never lost, it seems, the sense of this light even in the darkest or, in her case, the most confusing moments. It seems to me to have been a minor miracle, a personal miracle that reveals what the universe gave her, what it loaned her, to be more specific as a custodian of the light that she has been permitted to pass on to others.

To be a healer of Eileen's caliber means to be as undefended as possible, to not only erect no barriers to the world of the imperfect self whenever possible, but to consciously take them down as they are discovered, to follow the scent, the fragrance of bravery, that says *go here, learn this, don't be afraid to start again.*

At one point in this book, Eileen writes:

> *After a lifetime of healing, meditation, prayer, and other spiritual practice, I have realized that the Presence was never separate from me. Today, I feel the Presence inside of me and around me most of the time except when I get lost in some neurotic fearful place. And then I must stop and remember, that I am never too far away from the Presence, because it is inside of me and around me.*

Please note this passage for two things. The first is that she has contact with this Presence and knows that it exists both within her and around her. This means it is not self-generated by her egoic self. She doesn't claim ownership of it but rather *partakes of it* in a genuine way. But, more importantly to me, is the passage that starts with the words *except when I get lost in some neurotic fearful place.*

In this day, when self-aggrandizement is the norm, and therefore the least trustworthy part of people we are trying to trust, this statement, nakedly honest and undefended, means that here is a person who knows something about what it means to be a truly spiritual being, a perfectly imperfect being who can—spiritually speaking—shake hands with each person she meets and helps because she does not have territory to defend but only heart to share. And that, to me, is another one of Eileen Marder-Mirman's essential qualities: she's willing to go the extra mile. As her teacher and now, her dear friend, I have been the recipient of her generosity many times. Her attitude toward this type of giving? *Of course! That's the way it is!* It is never articulated that way but felt that way because it comes naturally to her. It fills her soul.

Eileen is willing to walk into anything. As you go through this book, following the trail that Eileen walked to become who she is today, her essential goodness comes to the reader front and center. It did for me. To follow a good person, a real person, a struggling person, and watch her emerge from shock to splendor, is an amazing thing. Please walk with her and be inspired. Then your heart and her heart can meet and share. That is the greatest healing there is.

Jason Shulman, Founder, A Society of Souls

INTRODUCTION

As a psychotherapist and a healing teacher, I have met and worked with hundreds of professional women (and men) over the past 45 years. Many of them have struggled with not knowing how to fully express their authentic selves and live life on their own terms.

They knew that there was more to life than what they were experiencing, they just didn't know what it was or how to feel connected to themselves and others in an honest way.

How can I be my true self?

I'm successful in life, so why do I feel so unhappy?

Why do I feel like something is missing?

Does being who I truly am mean I have to destroy everything I created?

I don't tell you how to live, I tell you what I have done, how I found myself and embraced my imperfections so that I can be in relationship with people just where they are.

As a child, I unconsciously developed a powerful manifesto: *Don't be who you are; stay safe and hidden at all costs.*

There was one significant problem — I always knew something wasn't right.

When the stars finally aligned, I gave myself permission to wake up to this truth...**How I Think I Should Be is B***S***.**

Once I understood that, I refused to spend any more time cocooned within a false sense of safety. My decision was clear, so I rolled up my sleeves and set out on my journey to awakening.

Even so, this journey was not easy. I had no idea how to be myself.

I began by questioning everything. I turned my beliefs on their head and inside out. I learned that by being honest with myself and developing a real and truthful relationship with all my inner parts, I could begin to transform.

The paths were many: vision quests, gurus, psychotherapy, energy healing, creativity, knitting, hiking, and plant medicine, to name a few. Each experience taught me something about myself and about the world and offered me new insights. Each place was a portal into my truest self.

Remembering my story was the gateway that allowed my broken parts to be touched and held by me. As I gave my shattered parts a place inside my mind, body, and spirit, I realized that by being present with my own open heart I could inhabit my true home.

Ever so carefully, I entered secret crevices, I uncovered exiled emotions, I discovered my heartbreak. I entered my body in a new way. Believe it or not, there was more freedom here. Touching and growing into a real relationship with my shadow side felt both frightening and enlivening.

I swam in an ocean of tears. I wept for the "me" who had been lost in the darkness. As I shed all the layers of protection, I'd wound around myself — my fear, my anger, and my arrogance — I realized that the more I embraced my emotional pain and suffering, the wider my heart opened. It wasn't easy. Yet each piece I healed offered me another level of freedom.

It took me many years and much work before I realized that the answers to many of life's questions lived hidden inside of my heart.

Today, I can rest in my truth: I am already whole and simultaneously I have frailties, imperfections, and limitations. I don't have to be perfect. I am fine just the way I am. And I am committed to love myself and others with all my heart and soul.

This memoir is my way of sharing my deepest realizations. I bring my experiences to you. I bring the map of the territory I traversed through the dark and the light to you. My prayer is that it will inspire you to become more of your imperfect, real, compassionate, and authentic self and help you navigate the beauty and suffering of this uncertain, imperfect, strange, and crazy life.

Since we likely can't speak 1-on-1 about this, this book is my gift to you. And I hope you will join in the movement against the bullshit that people say we have to be.

May you be blessed.
Eileen

1

BORN WITH FORCE

*"Tell me, what is it you plan to do with
your one wild and precious life?"*

~Mary Oliver

N o choice. I was ready. As I made my descent into
the world, the gurgling contractions were innately
ripe. With no warning of any kind, I was violently
taken from my warm oceanic home with a terrifying and
disorienting cold foreign object. It forced its way next to me
and wrapped around my soft, vulnerable head and developing brain. My natural rhythm aborted. Sensing the next
moment was no longer possible. All inherent instinctive
knowing was exiled.

Welcome to the world.

No love, no gentle holding, no consideration for my
sweet, naked, little fragile body, no awareness that I was
traumatized, no connection with my mother who was
drugged to not feel pain. I was handed off to a stranger who
obediently did her duty; it was a cold, sterile room. Nothing
holy, no warmth, no shimmering.

No heart connection, only shock, disorientation, pain, and suffering.

These unnatural moments were imprinted into my body, my pre-verbal mind, and my spirit. Newborns need to bond with the people they meet at birth. Did I bond to the doctor? Or to the nurse? Did I bond with anyone?

Mom's lack of consciousness during the actual birthing process affected me. Being drugged before I was born affected me. The doctor's need to get this done in his time flowed into me. Being taken from my mother affected me. Nurses scurrying about and quickly cleaning me up flowed into me.

It is amazing that I was able to thrive.

It was standard birthing protocol in Manhattan, New York hospitals in 1954 — drug the mother so she doesn't feel pain, forcefully pull the baby out with forceps, and have the father stay alone in the waiting room. Nothing natural. All controlled. Outrageous!

According to the medical journals I could access, the protocol to drug the birthing mothers and use forceps for births during 1954 was to help doctors speed up the birthing process. There was no scientific reason why this should have been done. Also, often there was tremendous trauma to the infant — brain damage, cerebral palsy, and death. And many mothers suffered from a lifetime of incontinence along with other uterine and vaginal conditions.

And then there was this.

Throughout his life, my father told me the story of how the nurse brought me out so he could meet me and hold me after I was cleaned up. He reveled in the fact that he was the first to hold me. I was loved and wanted. I believe that love and my profound early connection to spiritual presence is what sustained me throughout my life.

Manhattan, New York, 1954. Eisenhower was president, Leonard Bernstein was conducting at Carnegie Hall, *Damn Yankees* and *Peter Pan* were on Broadway. Hope, creativity, passion, and prosperity filled the air.

Not a bad time to be born.

New York City had finally overcome the Great Depression and was reshaping itself from the ravages of World War II. The flood of survivors and refugees through Ellis Island ended. New York was becoming a financial mecca, European artists migrated to Manhattan, the manufacturing businesses and factories sprouted up all over the five boroughs of New York City.

After my parents married in 1950, they lived with my maternal grandparents in a two-bedroom apartment on the Upper West Side. It was a special part of the city; it was a Jewish enclave and refuge with lots of European refugees.

At that time, my young parents' understanding and belief about life was immature and undeveloped. They easily fell into subjugation with doctors who they saw as "all powerful and wise." They completely gave their power over to the doctor, it was certainly a time of ignorance and appeasement for two intellectuals.

Women had very few rights in 1954, even in the prosperous, artistic, spirited world of New York City. Women were not thought of as equal; they were fearful of what others would think if they were successful in a man's world — medicine, law, university professorship, and more.

Women also had their place as caretakers who oversaw the family and household. They were able to work but it was an ancillary thing. Most women were not held in high esteem. The world was vastly different then, even though there are still artifacts of inequality and lack of respect today in 2023.

Most employers had mandatory leave policies requiring women to leave work upon reaching a certain month of pregnancy; mom hid the fact that she was pregnant with me for as long as she could. She often told me how she had to hide her body. Her anxieties and concerns about being found out flowed into me.

There was so much unconsciousness and fear.

Believe it or not, this was the medical advice that the obstetrician gave to my mother: limit weight gain and restrict your food intake. Unbelievable! I am sure that my parents had a top-level obstetrician from Columbia University Hospital since Dad graduated from Columbia University's dental school later that year.

Honestly, I can't imagine how she did that, to follow the doctor's orders. During my pregnancy in 1983-84, in the 2nd and 3rd trimesters, I craved certain foods, I mean craved! It felt physiological although I imagine there was anxiety entwined within the cravings. I had to eat several times a day and I ate whatever my cravings dictated.

So, here's the deal: having encountered lack of nutritional nourishment in utero and being victim to a forceful birth left deep scars in my body, mind, heart, and spirit.

The severe nutritional restrictions and my mother's unconscious emotional turmoil during my gestation resulted in a lifetime of gastrointestinal struggles, food sensitivities, and confusion around nourishment.

My body stored physical and emotional pain. Pain was just a part of my life.

As a very young child, I dealt with the pain mostly by ignoring it as much as possible. And being a sensitive little girl, I picked everything up that people weren't acknowledging and yet I had to separate myself from it.

Somehow, I taught myself how to ignore the pain, as it was just too much. It was easier to live in my own inner hidden world. It was what it was and that was that. I developed a high level of tolerance for pain. Hold it in, stay safe at all costs. Don't live fully, don't be myself fully. That was my unconscious motto.

No one knew how much pain I was in.

Isolated and misunderstood, my sensitivity was exponential on all levels, physically, emotionally, mentally, and psychically. Over the years I developed a keen sense of hypervigilance. I was able to "know" when I was safe and when I wasn't.

There was so much holding and "stuckness" in my body that I didn't learn how to breathe properly until my first yoga class in 1973. It was a miracle indeed. I held a trauma reaction in my body for years. Talk about the freeze response in trauma, it was so familiar that it felt innate. The freeze response is an automatic patterned response to a perceived threat and the unconscious inner protection goes into survival mode, neither running away nor fighting. And thankfully it wasn't innate or a natural way of responding to the world. Thankfully, it was healable.

So, this is how it all started. This was my beginning.

2

MOTHERING

"Sometimes the strength of motherhood is greater than natural laws."

~ Barbara Kingsolver

For more than a decade — and probably for many lifetimes — my heart longed to be open and real. Birthing my son and becoming a mother was a supersonic portal into a foreign and yet oh-so-familiar land. Nothing woke me up faster. Mothering and now, grand-mothering have been my greatest joys and blessings.

We were living the hippish bohemian-turned-yuppy life, working as two young naïve professionals in Manhattan. My husband and I always wanted to have children; it was a no-brainer. We had been married for four wonderful years filled with travel, loving, studying, working, and exploring life; Sunday morning *New York Times*, Saturday night foreign films, and so much more.

It was our fourth anniversary; we were dining at a lovely restaurant on the East River. Suddenly there was a quivering, a fluttering; sort of like internal fireworks I had never felt before. I knew in that moment that I was pregnant.

My husband's sperm swam upstream and fertilized my egg that was looking for its mate — it was a miracle.

Back in those days, we had to go to a laboratory and have a blood test. There weren't any pregnancy tests from the drugstore. Birthing centers were popping up in Manhattan and a lot of women were giving birth at home. I was a bit anxious about going to a birthing center or having a home birth, so I opted to use a wonderful obstetrician on 5th Avenue and 11th street who had midwives in her practice. It was the best of both worlds. The practice afforded me the kindness, compassion, and support I craved.

My heart was full; I already loved him.

As a pregnant woman, my inner knowing, and all my senses were intensified. I was so connected to myself and my growing baby, it seemed like the most natural thing in the world even though I looked sort of like an alien with this great big baby growing, eating, developing, being, and kicking inside of me. The miracle of being able to help create and be the conduit for a child to grow in and through me was awe inspiring.

There was an enhancement of all my senses and relationships. I felt more connected to my husband, my family, and my spiritual life.

There was this depth in the connection I felt with the baby when I was pregnant and afterwards that went beyond any other connection I had ever known.

I knew that whatever I ate, whatever I felt, whatever I didn't feel, whatever I knew, the love, the fear, the happiness, the presence, the breaths I took, and the fun I had philosophizing about life as a mother, all flowed into my womb and into my baby. He was growing and flourishing.

For nine months I connected to him, praying, singing, talking to him, dreaming with him, reading to him, meditating, philosophizing, walking the streets of NYC with him. Having my child growing in my body was miraculous, I knew I was blessed.

During the pregnancy I was often up at night — it's not uncommon to have some sort of insomnia while pregnant since after all pregnancy brings this profoundly bizarre physically huge change and ushers in change on every level. When I couldn't sleep, I sat in the living room gazing out of the large row of windows onto 27th Street while my husband was asleep in the room next door.

It isn't easy to sleep when pregnant, every organ was smooshed into various crevices of my body so that the baby could thrive. I was cocooned by the quiet Manhattan nights when most of the city was asleep. I knew with all my heart that I was entering a new life. And of course, some of what kept me up was my anxiety.

We were going from being the two of us in a small apartment with a dog to three of us with a dog. Everything was completely new, exciting, and unknown. All I knew for sure was that our hearts were in the right place.

My heart, luck, destiny, or karma — who knows exactly what it is that brings us together with our kindred spirits — mysteriously guided my husband and I together. Five plus years later, after having been two wild, young lovers "living the life" in our beloved Manhattan, we were truly blessed with the birth of our son.

After nine months of gestating and growing our baby, going to the midwife and my ob-gyn for monthly checkups and a few tests — there weren't that many to take back then — we gave birth to our son, Josh, on May 3, 1984. My husband was by my side taking pictures, my parents, and my Nanny Fritze were all with us in Beth Israel hospital, which was progressive in those days.

Counting his teeny fingers and those perfect little toes, smelling his new fresh aroma, nursing when he was hungry and lonely, changing him, and soothing him, brought me into an alignment with the reality that I had experienced here and there through my young adult years. It brought me to a place where I knew that the divine was present right there in that very moment and not somewhere far away that I had to reach by being different from how or where I was. I was completely my imperfect young mother self, being present and awake to the best of my ability. I can see why people have many children, as there is a direct link to a spiritual feeling of belonging, of the miraculous, of the mystery, of love and connectedness that has taken me decades to experience as a meditator and spiritual seeker. That feeling of being present here in this life and wrapped up in a blanket of life, love, meaning, and purpose was awesome.

That most precious time together definitely set the foundation for the incredible relationship we have today. So many surprises, so much to learn.

And nursing, that was the most intimate thing I have done in my life. My body, my breasts, the rich milk I created, all were the source of his nourishment and life. My soul was the nourishment for his soul. Quickly, I began to realize that I needed to keep nourishing my body, heart, and soul to truly nourish his.

Before motherhood, it was about attaining and feeling safe. After giving birth my heart burst open with a universal sense of being, belonging, and knowing. Some of what showed up for me in those first few months of mothering made me a far greater person than I could have ever imagined.

Becoming truly authentic was my first choice on the menu. I started to discover a newfound uncertainty, an allowance for imperfection, and an inner empowerment. They became my heart's companions as I traversed the new me, new life, and new relationship with the world.

It took time to adjust to my new life; being a mom and having this beautiful precious little being with me completely dependent on me for life, food, health, and well-being. I took my new job seriously. It wasn't always easy, it challenged me to grow and wake up in ways that I prayed for and in ways that I had never imagined.

Life became clearly delineated: before mothering and then mothering. I was turned upside down and inside out. I wobbled around for a while until I realized that I needed to take care of myself so I could take care of this baby who needed me. And I needed to learn what that meant.

I knew that life would be different; the me that I knew would shape-shift into a mother and the young married non-mother would be a part of my past. We had been married for five years then and I never felt as committed to life and my marriage as when I became a mother.

We became a family instead of a son and daughter-in-law or a daughter and son-in-law. We had our own little world and bubble with just the three of us. It was divine. Everything was divine, challenging, and unknown, and it didn't matter. I loved mothering and wife-ing.

I was completely passionate and committed to being the best, most loving mother. I longed to nourish him physically, emotionally, mentally, and of course spiritually.

It was a quiet early morning, shortly after Josh was born. We moved to the suburbs into a small cape-style home. My husband had already left to take the Long Island Railroad to go to work to support our little family.

As I did many times throughout the day, I was nursing the baby in our bed and gazing out the window. I was as present as I could be at 29. I was glowing in the light of something larger than myself that was created through my love and passion and his joy of receiving and being loved.

Out of somewhere, I heard a loud inner voice saying, "I can kill." I was shocked.

Suddenly instead of feeling like a vulnerable young mother, I was flooded with a sense of empowerment that I rarely had allowed myself to experience in the past. I saw myself as a tigress that could and would kill to protect my precious child. But more than that, I could and would kill, period! I was shaken, and simultaneously relief was entwined within my shaky foundation.

Even though it was scary to wake up and realize that I can kill and would kill, it was liberating. I was ready and open.

I had prayed to be my true self for years and all of that meditating and those vision quests brought me to a place where mothering was able to open me into developing an honest relationship with all of me.

I was shocked awake, and it was just another beginning.

3

LOSS

*"Before you know kindness as the deepest thing inside,
you must know sorrow as the other deepest thing."*

~Naomi Shihab Nye

I n a flash, loss and grief changed me and the course of my life. I had a plan. I was on a path, and it was all going well. I had it all mapped out, I was the captain of my ship.

Unprepared, my plan shattered and the whole trajectory of my life changed.

So much for making plans and thinking I knew how life would go and how it should go. That whole way of thinking was a fantasy and completely split off from reality. I plummeted into the depths of sorrow when my plans burst into flames.

I didn't realize that from meeting my pain and my suffering I would grow and flourish. I would no longer be the same. That was a hard fact to swallow. There was a wisdom in me, it whispered to me and let me know to keep on trucking. Somehow, I knew from deep within my heart and my soul about every step that I needed to take even though some were mistakes.

About 18 months after our son was born, we decided to have another child. Just like that, as if there were a guarantee. So, we got pregnant again easily. I was so happy to be pregnant again; we loved being parents so much and wanted to have three children.

Everything was going well.

Suddenly, 4 1/2 months later, I miscarried. We had had an early miscarriage before the full-term pregnancy with Josh. We were told that was common with first pregnancies, so we didn't make much of it. But during the second trimester, that was a different story. Frankly, I was horrified and shocked. And having a D&C was another trauma. Are you kidding me, it was so unnatural. But I was naïve about the healthiest path to take in such a situation and so was everyone else close to me.

Miscarriage, no reasons, no one to talk to, no answers, no internet, no books, only questions and devastating loss and physical trauma. Thankfully, I was already going to a heart centered psychotherapist who supported me and my vulnerability so I could be there for myself and the baby.

I didn't know anything about miscarriages and nobody else seemed to as well, not even the fancy Manhattan doctors. We were tested and went to this doctor and that specialist; they couldn't find anything wrong and so we suffered through 4 miscarriages.

So many people said that everything happens for a reason. So, what's the reason? Maybe that's true. Maybe it's not true and there is no reason. Maybe it just was what it was and nothing more.

What I did know was that I was grief-stricken and experienced loss in a way that was disheartening.

I was angry, I was devastated, I looked to blame, I judged and questioned myself at every turn. Always looking for a reason for the unexplainable. I was told there was no reason and that it happens all the time. Hmm, not helpful.

There was something wrong, they just didn't know what it was!! It turned out that I just needed more progesterone, a hormone that supports pregnancy!

I was in the unknown in a way I had no training for. My heart was heavy, I just wasn't the same.

At first, I attempted to make meaning out of everything to try to feel better and fix my broken heart. I was trying to erase the loss and trauma. But of course, that was like being a gerbil in a cage with no exit.

Was it my fault? Did I do something wrong? Does it mean that I really didn't want to have another baby? Does it mean that I did too much of this and too much of that? Or not enough of this and not enough of that? Was I a bad person in a past life and was this the pay back?

In some crazy way, the self-doubt and self-torture at every breath helped me to not feel the depth of my sorrow.

Mostly, I focused on mothering and wife-ing, friends and family. The changes that I went through brought me closer and closer to what I had prayed for my whole life. I wanted to be more real and a compassionate mother, therapist, woman.

Sometimes I ran away from my feelings. I always meditated. I became involved in new age thinking, I soaked in inspiring books, I returned to working part time, and I engaged with tons of knitting, quilting, and crafting. I often felt alone and beyond my ability to stay centered.

My plans and concepts about life were shattered. I was standing on shifting sands and catapulted into a subterranean land that was only partially lit. Nothing was familiar, nothing known, no control, no signs saying which way to go. I knew I was alive although death and a dimly lit path were my guides.

It wasn't just losing pregnancies; it was losing a whole life plan that was pulled out from under me without any suspicion of danger or warning. My whole life's trajectory shifted. I was more and more real, present and alive. There was a paradoxical healing that I was immersed in and didn't realize for a while. As I embraced that discombobulating and grief-stricken place, I was scared. But more than anything, I wanted to create a good life filled with love and now loss too. I became more compassionate from traversing this territory. I became a better mom, wife, and human. Slowly I accepted my faults and my desires as I learned about and developed a relationship with each part of myself.

I refused to allow the tremendous losses to stop me from being the best version of myself.

Being willing to feel like I was walking through the desert with very little water but my husband and a child and a dog or cat by my side healed me.

Psychotherapy, not being alone with my losses, being willing to be with the unknown, allowing myself to grow through the ashes like the Phoenix rising, not being fake, being willing to wake up and be real and honest even though it wasn't always easy — all made a difference and opened my heart.

The new unknown land and my uncertainty informed me as I developed an ability to be with it for longer periods of time and not crash from it.

I found spiritual and therapeutic processes that softened my broken heart, integrated my uncertainty so I wasn't so shaky and refreshed my longing for happiness.

Even though I felt victimized, fragile, and incomplete, I absolutely refused to stay a victim.

I dove into my fears and my pain. I allowed my agony, I journaled, I talked about it, I remembered what I was grateful for, I loved, I mothered, I wifed, I daughtered, I sistered, I aunted, I friended, I healed.

All this slowly brought me home to my whole awakening heart.

Loss has been my teacher. I am no longer afraid of it. Now I know that part of the fabric of life is to live and to lose and to live with loss.

As I held my heavy, broken heart closer and closer, I learned how to mother myself. I allowed myself to mourn because I needed to.

I refused to allow these tremendous losses to stop me from being the best mother and best version of myself as possible. It was hard to let go of the idea and our plan of having 3 children. After many years, a tidal wave of tears and a mountain of rage, I moved on.

One thing that helped to save me through all the losses was that my husband, Jamie, was always by my side.

Even though I am 68 years old, and I have traversed a lot of inner territory, and I have healed a lot through my losses, I still feel loss when loss arises. I know this territory well. Sometimes I am still terrified of it and most of the time it just sits within my heart.

4

THE PRESENCE

"The one that I long for is always here,
I just have to open my heart...."

At night, when the world was asleep, I often woke up in the wee hours of the morning. Gently rising from my bed, I gazed out the window of my bedroom, located at the front of the house on the second floor. I could see straight down the tree-lined Clinton Lane, the street that ended in front of my childhood home at 41 Orange Drive, Jericho, New York.

I gazed and gazed and gazed.

The place that I called home, and the surrounding environs became so spacious and expansive. Glistening stars, the surprise of shooting stars, the clouds billowing; the entire night sky filled me.

I entered a nothingness that was so full the Presence held me close. It was quiet and peaceful except for the streetlamps that made gentle, whistling sounds.

The Presence drew me there night after night. There was something comforting in the velvety darkness. I was safe.

Mostly, I was the silence of the snow after a storm, and I was not alone.

The cacophony of the birds and the insects in the early morning before sunrise guided me back to dreamland as the milkman journeyed in his little cart-like truck to each home in our neighborhood.

The Presence of the night sky was my refuge, my saving grace. And all mine.

It was 1959; I was 4 1/2 years old. We had moved from the comfort of my grandparent's apartment on West 94th Street in Manhattan, New York to Forest Hills, to Flushing, and then into a home on Long Island in one of those communities with mostly first and second generation young families of Jewish and Italian descent. The Long Island Expressway was not complete. There were piles and piles of soil for the builders to construct more homes just beyond our small parcel of land and home.

We walked quietly to the synagogue, the building where the Jewish community gathered. My little hand happily was held by his large, strong hand as we crossed the many streets en route to our destination. I was the cute, lucky little girl all dressed up with the tall, handsome, smart father. I was so proud to be with him.

At first, Jericho Jewish Center was in a huge tent; the neighborhood was not fully developed in 1959 and most of the people who lived there were World War II veterans and were able to buy their homes inexpensively because of the GI bill. What is now a neighborhood of upper-middle-class and upper-class Long Islanders was settled by a group of middle-class families of veterans. It took a while for them to have enough funds to construct the beautiful synagogue that I loved dearly. Most of the congregation was comprised of immigrants from Eastern Europe and a few families of first-generation Americans like mine, since my family on both sides emigrated in the late 1800's.

It was a very special time for me. I completely adored my father and loved going to services with him; I sat in the sanctuary right next to him, my feet not able to touch the ground. The men and a few women davened and prayed as they read aloud in Hebrew and sometimes in English. The air smelled and felt exactly like the Presence of the night, it was living right there in the synagogue! The illumination of holiness filled the sanctuary. I belonged. The melodies of the songs warmed my heart and transported me to little villages in Eastern Europe. Each time I heard the songs, I felt connected to my ancestors as if I were a thread in a tapestry of ancient Judaism. Today, I still love singing the tunes and the harmonies even when I can't remember all the words.

In the front of the sanctuary, there was a bimah, a platform where the rabbi led the service, and the cantor sang the liturgical music and a few others sat and stood. Magnificently handcrafted stained-glass windows surrounded the sanctuary, picturing the Twelve Tribes of Israel.

And then, there was the ark, the place where the holy *Torah*, the five books of scripture that were revealed to Moses, was housed. It was covered with dark velvet curtains. There was some sort of symbol embroidered on it.

There is a sacred prayer that is sung announcing the opening of the Ark.

A chosen honored member of the congregation would carefully, precisely and with deep reverence, open the doors to the ark and the curtains covering the *Torah*. The *Torah* would be taken out ever so carefully. The ritual was filled with respect and holiness.

The *Torah*, the Five Books of Moses, was made of parchment and calligraphed in Hebrew; the *Torah* was rolled on wooden dowels and there were silver ornaments hanging on it. When it was opened to a specific page for that day, I could see it glowing — it was and is other worldly. I breathed in the glow. The *Torah* is traditionally the center of the Jewish community. It is usually adorned and even though not all Jewish people are religious or even traditional, the religious objects represent the lineage that has been passed down through the centuries.

In the sanctuary, I was transported into the realm of life that I touched every night by myself. The holiness wrapped me in a depth of splendor; the prayers of anguish, longing, and devotion touched my little heart and soul. I was home.

I wanted more of it, so I went to Hebrew school, but the teacher was creepy, the class was almost all boys, and I felt like I didn't belong. I dropped out of the Hebrew school and went to Yiddish school which was named after Sholom Aleichem—the writer whose short stories led to the show *Fiddler on the Roof* and many other tales of Jewish life in Eastern Europe.

Even though the rabbi and the cantor were always men back in those days, I felt at home and at peace. I belonged to a long lineage of Jewish people. I was aware, however, that there weren't too many women or girls in the sanctuary during the early hours of the services.

For a good part of my life, I experienced the Presence as separate from me and something I longed for. The Presence surrounded me and helped me to know that I was not alone and was loved.

After a life of healing, meditation, prayer, and other spiritual practices, I have realized that the Presence was never separate from me. Today, I feel the Presence within me and around me most of the time except when I get lost in some neurotic fearful place. And then I must stop and remember, that I am never far away from the Presence since it is within me and around me.

The One that I long for is always here. I just have to open my heart, take a breath, pause, and remember. The Presence has been one of my blessings.

5

LINEAGE

*"To forget one's ancestors is to be a brook without a source,
a tree without a root."*

~Chinese Proverb

"*Remember us. As you heal, you heal us. We stand behind you and the future is yet to come. Be who you are and not what you thought you had to be.*"
There is an invisible thread, a collective unconsciousness, that's beyond space and time that connects me to my family's lineage. The past wafts by like a slide show. I am a part of the web that is made of this ancestral memory. I can feel and perceive these places and images as if it's in my recent memory. I used to ignore their voices but now I pay attention, open my heart, and say, yes, I am here.

I am carrying forward the history of the mothers and the fathers who have come before me through my genes, my love of family, and through the suffering which I am devoted to healing into its original form of wholeness. My heart's desire and intention bring a shimmering to the darkness of this human existence. May we all be blessed by tikkun olam— the healing and repair of the world.

The miracle of surviving slavery in Egypt, living through the diaspora and having to leave homeland after homeland, leaving everything behind, surviving plagues, pogroms, along with an attempt to eradicate the Jewish race, is what I carry in my soul.

It was January in the late 1980's, and we had finally saved enough money to fly the 3 of us to Israel to visit my brother, sister-in-law and their then 5 children for 3 weeks. In those days, we were not given a definite time when the flight would take off. At JFK airport, we had to go through several security checks and take a tram that bused the passengers to an unknown destination at the airport. I was filled with excitement and an awareness of danger.

Military jeeps accompanied our flight down the runway. We were off to another land, the land of our ancestors. Thirteen hours later we landed at Ben Gurion Airport near Tel Aviv. It was snowing in Jerusalem and the Israeli-Palestinian conflict was fairly calm for the moment.

When I stepped off that EL AL flight and took a breath of that fresh desert winter air, I felt I had come home. Home to a place I had known deep inside my consciousness somehow.

We drove along modern-day roads north of Tel Aviv and Haifa and ascended the curved roads that brought us to the old city of Zefat (Safed), a seat of Kabbalah, mystical Judaism, in the 1500's.

The narrow, winding cobblestone streets were lined with cafes, ancient homes, and art galleries. Each had a mezuzah on the doorpost at the entrance. Mezuzahs contain a parchment scroll with a blessing, *"and thou shall write them upon the doorposts of thy house and on thy gates,"* found in the *Book of Deuteronomy.*

It was a joyful time. The children were young, and we had a pizza party in the small hotel. We went from gallery to gallery; the children ran around, and we all stopped by a woman making fresh juice outside. We made her day! So much joy. And I was with the loves of my life.

The holiness of this hilltop village shimmered through the air as I was transported back to another time. I felt deeply connected, to the land, the sounds, the smells, the people, my family, and life.

In some unseen mystical way, I felt as if I had never left this place. It is inscribed in my soul and my heart.

Prayer oozed from the stones and swayed in the air. We walked by the small humble stone homes of many of the Kabbalistic rabbis of years past; Isaac Luria, Moses Cordovero, Joseph Caro, and Chaim Vital.

Embedded in every life and every family are secrets, lies, and betrayal. And some families, like in mine, also have love that infuses and surrounds everyone along with the suffering. Secrets and unconscious traumas are passed down mother to daughter, mother to son, father to daughter and father to son and so on. We are all so deeply connected in ways that are beyond comprehension, to all of humanity, to every living and non-living thing and beyond.

My family lineage is made up of all those ingredients, it is sort of a stew: take the unconsciousness from this side of the family and add it to the other side of the family and each child is born into that transgenerational matrix. We are profoundly affected on all levels by those who have come before us.

In the late 70's, I went to a conference on suicide at the World Trade Center in lower Manhattan. The building shook as we sat there way above the city. To maintain my status as a clinician I needed to take all sorts of courses. Some of them were interesting and supported my desire to learn more and incorporate more into the work that I offered to my clients; some of it was unfulfilling.

The workshop started with a survey about who we knew in our family that had committed suicide. I said no one. Emphatically, they said, every family has suicide in it and since suicide is so toxic and poisonous it seeps into the family in hidden ways and affects everything and everyone, not just the immediate survivors of the one who commits suicide.

Not me, I could not relate at all to what they were saying but I took it in anyway and felt disturbed by it.

That evening, I met my grandmother for dinner. I told her about the conference and how they said that every family has suffered from a loved one's suicide. She said, yes, that's true, in our family as well. One of her sisters had committed suicide. I was dumbfounded as well as shocked.

It was a secret and for the first time in my 25 years of life, she spoke of it with such ease as if it were the most natural thing to talk about. I guess she thought I was ready to know.

She didn't understand how the effects of the suicide and the secrets surrounding would be passed through the family. I told her how it affects close family members and when not processed at all, the trauma gets passed down. It affects everything.

Uncle Gerry, my father's eldest brother, was stationed in Germany in World War II in Patton's battalion. He was a fun-loving uncle and he an incredible reader. I remember all those books piled up on the floor of his room lining the walls like another layer of wallpaper. He often stayed with my brother and me when my parents went out of town. I truly loved him.

In 1976, he was in Lenox Hill Hospital and the doctors erroneously told the family that he didn't have long to live. I was very close with Uncle Gerry so after I hung up the phone with Dad, I booked a flight to New York.

When I arrived in his room, he told me he wanted to tell me something that he hadn't told anyone before (it turned out others knew about this). I thought I was going to say good-bye and then instead he shared the story of a broken heart that he had been carrying for years.

He had fallen in love with a German Christian woman during World War II when he was stationed in Germany. He loved her dearly, but she was Christian and German, and this love was forbidden by my Jewish family, especially in light of the Holocaust.

One day when he went to visit his girlfriend, he discovered blood all over the floor in the entryway. She had undergone an illegal abortion. He was devastated. He contemplated staying in Germany, even knowing that he would never be accepted back into his family again.

His mother, my grandmother — not my favorite person — threatened him and said that she would kill herself by putting her head inside an oven if he stayed with the girl.

Once back in New York, he tried to fall in love with other women, but he never could. He never received any support for what was called post World War II "battle fatigue syndrome," now known as post-traumatic stress disorder.

Uncle Gerry led a very sad life, filled with secrets, betrayal, religious controversy, fear, and deep loss. He suffered from the complications of diabetes for many years upon his return from the war and ended up living with my grandparents, taking care of them until their death. He never really lived his life. He left a part of his heart and soul in Germany.

He died alone in that apartment on the corner of Kings Highway and Ocean Parkway in Brooklyn from a diabetic coma. The lights in the world dimmed a bit when he left us.

What our ancestors lived and died for affects us. When they don't heal and create new relationships, that gets passed down to the next generation and then the next one and so on.

There's a beautiful Jewish tradition. When a baby is born, it is often named after a loved one who has passed, honoring the loved one and through a religious ritual the child is aligned with the lineage created 5,000 years ago. My mother's maternal family arrived in the United States in the late 1800's via boat from Galicia, near Russia, and settled in Shelton, Connecticut where they formed a farm. I was named for my mother's grandmother Eve, and I am not sure who I was named after with my middle name Leah — someone in one of the families. After they grew up, the children, my aunts and uncles, and my grandmother settled in the Bronx, not far from the promenade which was a type of Jewish enclave. I was very close with my nanny and her sister, Aunt Minnie.

My mother's paternal family settled nearby in New Haven, Connecticut, where we would go for holidays when I was quite young. I loved taking the car trip to Connecticut for the Jewish holidays until the time when my great-grandfather Abe died.

Yiddish is the Jewish language for Ashkenazi Jews, the sect of Jews from which I am a descendant. The family spoke it when we gathered for holidays and funerals. I always felt at home there even if I didn't understand all of what they were saying.

Every Sunday, we visited my maternal grandparents in the early afternoon for dinner. As we walked into the apartment building on Saunders Street in Rego Park, New York, the smells of roasted chicken and brisket wrapped me in a holy shawl. Even the smell of the old-fashioned elevator that would magically transport us to my Nanny and Papa's apartment smelled of a safe place. Nanny had little dishes filled with candy all over the place. Food was love. Candy was even better. Love, cozy, safe — except for the cigarette smoke and the quarrels in the bedroom on the other side of the apartment. Mostly, though, there was beauty, acceptance, and love.

It is profoundly touching to know how my ancestors struggled and wandered from their homeland time after time, suffered and brought forward the family so I can be here in this time and place.

I am eternally grateful. And there is healing.

6

WHO AM I?

*"Have patience with everything that remains
unsolved in your heart ... live in the question."*

~Rainer Maria Rilke

Who Am I? That's the ultimate existential question, isn't it? And, probably at the roots of philosophy. Ramana Maharishi, an Indian sage, created a self-inquiry practice. The practice is to make the inner awareness of "I" or "I am" as we intentionally inquire where it comes from.

Questioning about who I am started a long time ago and probably even before that.

In New York City in the 1950's, when many Jewish parents gave birth to a child, the child was given an American name and a Jewish name. My names are Eileen Lois and Chava Leah.

Eileen is traditionally an Irish name meaning bright and shining one, lively, pleasant, strength, little bird, and the desired one. And Lois, which is from the biblical Greek, means more desirable, better, or famous warrior.

In Hebrew, Chava means the first woman, the mother of all living. And Leah means delicate, weary and was also thought of as more contemplative and spiritual.

Naming is significant. It identifies us. It honors the past as we go forth into life. Even though I could not relate to these various aspects of my names for a long time, as I have healed, I am so much more embodied in who I am and all of my names.

Eileen Lois was an acceptable American name since it would not be evident that I was Jewish. It was a way to keep my Jewish heritage and culture hidden and keep me safe in the post-World War II world. It was about survival.

Naming gives us a place and yet I didn't experience being in one place. Having two sets of names was an out-picturing of the internal dissonance from which I suffered. I was split between me and myself.

As a young girl, I was the little, spiritual, delicate bird who was confused, shy, hidden, and weary. To the world, I was the bright, shining, lively, pleasant one. Later, I became a warrior.

The inner turmoil from which I suffered was not because I had two sets of names. The effects of a traumatic birth, struggle with internal physical and emotional sensitivities, and conflicts within the family lineage all created an environment that was tough to navigate.

I lived with so many questions. What made me behave and feel the way I did? Why was I struggling so much? What do I do with all these emotions? What is my purpose in life? Why am I here? How did I become the way I am? How can I change? How can I be who I know I am deep inside? Who am I?

As a teenager, I consciously began questioning who I was and who I was meant to be. The questions lived inside of me all the time. I loved when I met kindred spirits who wanted to talk about reality and explore the questions that had so much meaning to me. At summer camp, in the evenings, a group of us often sat outside under the stars philosophizing about life and our place in it. That was manna for my soul.

Growing up in a politically liberal family gave me a foundation for identifying with social justice. My parents held clandestine Democratic meetings in our home on Long Island; the curtains had to be pulled shut when the group gathered. It was a horrifying day when Allard Lowenstein, a U.S. representative for the 5th district in Nassau County, New York, was murdered. He spoke out about unpopular topics such as opposing the report about the death of Robert Kennedy and much more.

I identified with the ideology of the counterculture; peace, love, freedom, and longing to change the world. I couldn't tolerate violence in any form. I thought of myself as a "flower child."

As an undergraduate at Syracuse University, I majored in psychology and minored in anthropology. Clearly, I was searching for meaning and understanding.

I dove into the deep end. I was drawn to personality theories, social psychology, abnormal psychology, behavioral psychology, cultural anthropology, Russian literature, and science fiction.

As much as I loved my classes and what I was learning, it just wasn't enough. My small hippie soul-searching group of friends decided to explore reality through meditation, drugs, yoga, rock & roll, and hiking. I compulsively read books that supported the hippie movement and my awakening heart; Hesse, Heinlein, Brautigan, Kerouac, Tolkien, Kesey, Ram Dass, Huxley, Watts, everything about gestalt therapy, Castaneda, Trungpa, Buckminster Fuller, Black Elk, and Yogananda.

Simultaneously, I volunteered in the college women's center. *Our Bodies, Ourselves* by the Boston Women's Health

Collective, was my bible. It dared to talk about sexuality and abortions in a world that was still very anti-women's rights. Sadly, we still are struggling for women's rights today.

It was not easy to help women who are deciding whether to have an abortion, I was so young and ignorant and was just getting to find out about my own body. There was so much to learn. Thankfully, my heart was in the right place. Whenever I felt aligned with a "cause," I signed up.

The Westcott Café was a hippie granola-type cozy hang-out just outside of the university campus. For a semester or two, I volunteered to cook there twice a week. Somehow this type of work made me feel like a true part of the liberal, consciousness-raising culture at the university. It was good. Too bad I don't remember any of those creative pancake recipes I put together on those cold Syracuse mornings.

Creating our little community of friends was soul nourishment. It truly supported me in my awakening and healing. I was a part of something important, I belonged. We were soul sisters and brothers. Some of us have maintained contact over more than 45 years since graduation.

Then I entered graduate school to go deeper into psychological studies, completing a master's degree in counseling in 1977. I worked in the field and entered an intensive psychotherapeutic relationship for my personal healing. I remembered my historical story. I realized so much more of who I was and was born to be.

One day when I was in a psychotherapy session, I told my therapist I felt the way I perceived the world was upside down. She asked me to stand up, bend over and experience being in that upside-down state.

Yup, that's how it had felt for most of my life. To keep myself safe, there was so much I didn't share of what I saw, sensed, perceived, and knew.

There was something more I needed to explore and discover and I didn't know what it was. I moved on and went beyond psychotherapy, yoga, and sitting meditation.

Developing a relationship with the unknown, emptiness, uncertainty, imperfection, and impermanence and holding them close to my heart in a new way was the next stop.

Little did I know that healing the ego and not aiming to rid myself of it was going to be the revelatory part of my healing. Being inclusive of all that rose up in me was radically different as I discovered the spiritual teachings of Jason Shulman, the Founder of A Society of Souls, The School for Nondual Healing and Awakeningtm.

Through the wisdom of those studies, I included all my body, mind, heart, and spirit in a new way. It was a radical departure to walk directly into whatever rose in my consciousness whether it be physical sensations, emotional reactivity, mental confusion, or spiritual longings. I learned how to be more inside of myself and simultaneously with reality by entering into a universe that is the place where all opposites exist together, not as separate entities but as wholes. It was deeply healing. I felt more and more whole and real and less separate from myself, others, and the world.

As a teacher of Nondual Kabbalistic Healingtm, I came face to face with my limited self, time and time again. After all, I am this imperfect being who is committed and dedicated to the healing of each being and the world.

During the first year of the training, my co-teacher, Jeff Ellias-Frankel, and I offered a blessing circle during the last day of each weekend intensive. The class chants various names of the divine as we bless students. There is a glorious cacophony of voices. It is quite beautiful and touching.

How would I, the one who wanted to be the good, kind, loving, compassionate teacher, be worthy of blessing students? Clearly, I needed to do some soul searching; I needed to engage with lots of prayer and meditations. I was confused and once again in touch with a false belief about who I was!

When it was time, I opened my eyes and a student sat down in front of me. I asked her what she wanted a blessing for. She told me what she longed for and in that moment, I realized I just had to be myself.

Longing to bless and heal was the blessing.

Embodying my names has been an ongoing journey that has included forks in the road, black holes, the dark night of the soul, beautiful awesome landscapes, and the joy of presence in each moment. One day at a time and sometimes one moment at a time.

Spiritual practices, psychotherapy, physical healing too, but most of all putting my heart into life every day and every night even when the going gets tough.

7

WHY AWAKEN?

"Awakening is the birthright of every created being.
To know God is to know our destiny."

~Jason Shulman

What if awakening is becoming all of whom we are? And, what if awakening to our already-present contact with the divine wholeness and the real self is the healing?

Erroneously, I thought that healing and spiritual awakening was the result of achieving certain goals in meditation, chanting or other spiritual practices such as silencing the mind, eradicating the ego, or merging into the Oneness.

For eons, there were two parts of me in opposition.

Part of me was focused on staying safe. I wanted guarantees and to stay in control as if that were even possible. So, I stayed tight and asleep.

Part of me believed that I had to aspire to be a person who was free of the human frailties of life. I would be able to deal with even the most difficult of circumstances, free of emotions or any type of strife. I would be a type of super heroine. All dressed up with nowhere to go.

Bogged down in my personal feelings, with which I over-identified, I needed to realize that my philosophy of life was written from a split sense of self. I mean I was highly functioning in most ways, but I wasn't free. I was bound and contracted from a good deal of my truest, most tender self.

There was this other part of me that knew that I was not whole and that there was more to life than what I was living. I longed for more and I heard, felt, and sensed wholeness calling me closer. It was magnetic.

Passionately, I followed the scent all the way to the end and then to a new beginning and another end and another beginning. A true spiral of life and discovery.

Throughout my life, I have personally preferred light without darkness – I desired what is often described as a spiritual bypass that looked like this: world peace; the complete and eternal end of war and the elimination of all dissonance on this earth and of course inside of me.

The originators of Gestalt therapy left Austria after it became clear they were no longer safe to stay there when the Nazi presence got worse. Laura Perls wrote, "the demand for peace is in strict opposition to one of the most vital instincts of every living being, namely aggression."

What?! The part of me that identified with all my misconceptions wanted to run the other way. I wanted things to be shiny and beautiful with no aberrations at all. Those preconceptions and a mile-long list of demands I thought were realistic needed to dissolve. I no longer could tolerate feeling as if I were being thrown to the edge of a cliff each time a true difficulty showed up.

Laura Perls shocked me awake! Her thesis was that when we mold children into good little children and don't allow them to be wild animals, we create fascists. This made sense and it actually explained our present dilemma in the world with so much controversy, lack of consciousness, and the unwillingness to be in relationship with reality as it is.

I realized that I needed to rewire myself in more ways than I even thought was possible. It wasn't just about letting go or being grounded and balanced, it was about being authentic and allowing all the realness of the moment to be there as well as possible. To realize the false beliefs about who I was, what the world was, what the world needed to be, and how others needed to be was enlightening.

I had to traverse a lot of territory to get to the place of realizing the absolute importance of being in relationship deeply with the darkness and dissonance.

I was in the valley of longing to be.

My thinking was deluded. I thought that no good would or could come from experiencing what I deemed negative thoughts and feelings. That would mean that I was a bad person, and I would be exiled into a land all alone if I pursued the integrating of those aggressive forces. Part of me had no desire for victory. And well, you know, the other part of me only wanted victory.

This part of me believed that I shouldn't show my aggression. I was convinced that I needed to look a certain way as opposed to be whole and present in myself. And that completely affected my body and my mind in negative ways.

I knew in my heart of hearts that if I didn't do this work on becoming conscious of those aspects of myself that I would become destructive by projecting and acting out onto others and inward toward myself.

Now don't get me wrong, I had many peak spiritual experiences where I was whole and present in the moment. But they didn't last. My mission was to replicate them throughout the years. Until I realized that was an impossible and insane task.

I dreamt of finding Shangri-La where everything was in harmony. Then I would find the secret and enter the gates and I would transform into the idealized person that I believed I needed to become.

I know ... crazy right?

I didn't know that I needed to travel into the darkness and into myself to find the treasures waiting for me. Seriously, I thought I needed to find all the treasures outside of myself and bring them into me. So, I was constantly hunting for treasure – but rarely finding it.

I slowly walked through the arid desert, I explored the empty caverns, and I practically lost my life in the turbulent seas. But the land of the misty rains showed me the unburdening of my heart and the glimmering of light that arises after the storm.

As I was reclaiming myself, I began to understand what Buddhists have taught for milennia—be where you are. Something about this place was so familiar, I could breathe.

Why awaken? Awakening is the most natural thing we can do. We are all born with the call inside of us if we are just willing to listen. For millennia, I longed to wake up to the truth of reality and become who I was born to be.

That said, it has been an arduous path at times while simultaneously joy is part of my life, not separate from it.

So, life has been a blessing even though I have had to traverse a lot of darkness, loss, and despair. It all led to deeper and deeper states of realization and inner peace.

Walking directly into ambiguities and my brokenness healed me. I felt a sense of wholeness.

Thanks to the *Nondual Process of Conflict Resolution*, created by Jason Shulman, I was challenged with being able to be in relationship with disparate parts and to see that everything exists in light, even war.

For many years my belief about life was that everything needed to be filled with light and all nicey-nice. I now know this was a false belief that carried me until my arms and legs grew weary.

What I have learned:

There is a small voice that speaks to us if we dare to listen.

I had to wake up to my delusions.

I had to wake up to my split of being in the truth and being in a fairy tale.

As I became conscious of the obstacles I created, I developed a relationship with them and transformed into more of my true nature.

Looking back, I can see that the discomfort of not being in reality caused so much more suffering than waking up to the truth about who I am and what life is.

To heal and wake up takes a profound commitment to self.

Leaving no stone unturned, I found another part of my true nature waiting there to return to my heart.

To experience wholeness and reality as-it-is, I needed to be inclusive of the light and dark despite my preferences.

True freedom comes from being with the dissonances and difficulties and not getting rid of anything and being willing to develop a relationship with what we feared and that which we pushed away.

Awakening was all I ever wanted to do. I took many different twists and turns, and it was all to find some steadiness on my path called life. I became more of who I am, more real, more expressive, more honest, and more committed.

Learning to embrace the darkness of this world and not split from it, taught me that I had to heal my own darkness first.

I took responsibility for my thoughts and actions.

I woke up to what I knew and what I didn't know. That was a relief.

As I healed, I realized that God was not so far away and that we need companions on the path; we can't do it alone. Realizing that everything and everyone is interconnected and there is no separation was inspiring and restorative. Why awaken? Now I can be with things as they are in my imperfect, human way.

8

PRAYER

"Prayer is an attitude of the heart."

-Larry Dossey

As a young girl, my prayers were about beseeching and bargaining with a higher power. The prayers went something like this: *"Please if you help me with this, then I will do this or I will never do that again."* I was innocent as I bargained to receive help and be absolved of any wrongdoing.

Once I was at a birthday party at a roller-skating rink where there was a blue stuffed dog that was a prize. For some reason, I really wanted that dog. I remember talking to God and begging from the bottom of my heart about how much I wanted to win the prize – and I did. My prayer had been heard.

As a young adult, I still cried out for help to a higher power who knew what was best for me and could save me. I prayed when I felt alone, when I had something to figure out, when I struggled or when I needed support to help someone else.

And often at certain times of the year and for holidays, I engaged with a formal type of prayer, when I would recite from a sacred text. This helped me feel connected to my lineage as well as to God.

That said, prayer was not my go-to until my first trip to Israel in the late 1980's. Since then, my life has been infused with daily prayers. Something happened in Israel that woke me up.

It was the late 1980s. My brother and sister-in-law and their family had immigrated to Israel, and it took a few years for Jamie and me to save up enough money to fly the three of us to Israel for a never-to-be-forgotten experience.

We traveled all over Israel from the north to the south and from the east to the west. From their small apartment in a suburb of Tel Aviv to hotels all over the country and to kibbutzim.

We entered the Jaffa gate which is a portal into the old city of Jerusalem. The old city is walled within the modern-day Jerusalem. It was as if we had stepped into a time machine. Another world presented itself to us.

Everything and everyone were so incredibly alive, I was thrilled. People were hawking and trying to get us to buy tours, bread, this ornament, and that souvenir.

To the left was the narrow street leading into the Christian quarter. In front of us was an Arab shuk, a marketplace filled with tiny colorful stores carved into the stone with a narrow path descending into the Arab quarter.

On that first trip, we went to the right past the *Tower of David* and walked through and around the Armenian cobblestone streets. The spirit of antiquity is still completely present, in the rocks, in the walls, in the ramparts, in the little hovels, on the cobblestone streets, in the air, in the memory that fills you as you take each breath.

As we descended toward the Jewish Quarter and the Western Wall, there were remnants of Byzantine streets, there were burnt homes, ancient ruins and mosaics, yeshivas, columns, little children running around, artifact stores, a dog or a cat here and there scavenging for food and an old temple that had been in ruins and recently renovated.

There were cafes of all kinds, felafel, pizza, juice, dessert, and more. Life abounds in this large courtyard; I could sit there for hours.

Life and prayer were bound together, not separate from one another. My heart was glowing, and I was home.

As we continued the descent toward the Western Wall of the Temple, a feeling of awe and majesty filled me. I looked around at all the small apartments and yeshivas that surrounded the square. The holiness was palpable. In the distance was the golden dome of the rock, an Islamic shrine located on the Temple Mount in the Islamic quarter.

After we walked through the security section, my brother and husband went to the far end of the visible wall which is the men's area and I walked to the women's area. There were very poor women begging for money at the entrance into this sacred area. I always keep small amounts of money in my pockets to give to these women, they desperately need it. There are prayer books, siddurs, that many of the women use and rows of chairs.

Women were praying and crying and touching the wall, babies straddled between their legs, pieces of paper with prayers from visitors were sticking out of the cracks.

I waited to get closer to the wall so that I could touch it and pray. I placed the paper with prayers that I had brought from the United States from friends, family, and clients into the cracks in the wall where I was standing. I looked up; the wall was enormous. My heart expanded with each breath that I took.

As I touched the wall, I placed my forehead on it. I had no idea of what I would pray for or about. I had finally arrived at the Western Wall, often called the Wailing Wall, the place I had dreamt of and prayed to be at one day. Ecstasy!

Suddenly, it was no longer 1988. I could hear the sounds of chariots traveling over primitive roads made of stones. I had a sense that I was touching the wall of Solomon's Temple but had forgotten who the original creator of the temple was. As I touched it, I remembered.

King Solomon, the son of King David, completed the building of the Temple in 957 BCE, before the common era. The Ark of the Covenant lived there in a sacred chamber called the Holy of Holies. It was believed this was the most sacred place, where the Creator, the Intimate One, lived. The Temple was where Jewish life took place.

I could smell the dust and hear the horses neighing and the carts or chariots bumping atop the rocky roads. Had I been here before?

The air was filled with the holy Hebrew prayer of the Shema which can be transliterated: *Sh'ma Yisrael Adonai Eloheinu Adonai Ehad: "Hear, O Israel: the LORD is our God, the LORD is One."*

As I kept my forehead and hands on the Temple wall, the essence of the prayer surrounded me and deeply touched my heart. I started to recite it over and over.

The prayer was me and I was it, there was no separation.

I started to recite the *Shema* every day and every night. I learned about it and had it teach me. I started to say it silently before I offered a psychotherapy session.

My whole world, inner and outer, changed, and it was good. I felt more rooted, more present, and deeply connected to my lineage.

It was a summer weekend in 1996 when I enrolled in a *Kabbalah and Ecstasy* workshop with Jason Shulman at the *Omega Institute for Holistic Studies*. I had never heard of Jason.

Suddenly he was talking about his understanding of the *Shema*. My heart skipped a beat; holy moly!!

I had prayed for a spiritual teacher, I had tried this and that and more, and suddenly Jason was talking and teaching about a different understanding of the *Shema*. I started crying, had my prayers been answered?

Today, my life is permeated with prayer. I pray throughout the day. I sing my own prayers. I pray from a prayer book. I pray to remember my connection with divinity. I pray to heal, I pray for myself and my loved ones, I pray for wisdom. I pray for protection. And I pray to receive the blessings of the Creator.

Wherever I am, I pray from there. I often say the *Shema* and many times I use words of my own; either way I enter a new land that I call the space of prayer. I am different and transformed from this. I bring all of who I am into my prayers.

I hear my heart, I am vulnerable, I feel more whole, I am located in one place.

It's truly remarkable that through prayer, I've experienced a deep spiritual sense of connection to life as it is along with a personal experience of healing into more and more of my true self.

Through the years, when I have been devastated by loss, I have prayed to be supported and to not feel alone. And it made a difference; it is deeply healing.

In this place, I am wrapped in a shawl of Presence, healing, and awakening.

Prayer is an everyday refuge as I touch the soul of the interconnectedness of all.

9

RESCUE

*"Until one has loved an animal,
a part of one's soul remains unawakened."*

~Anatole France

I rescued them and they rescued me.
For as long as I can remember, I was captivated by the comings and goings of animals and other critters. Whether I was mesmerized by the scurrying about of sand crabs as I put sand in my pail to build little sand pies, or I was fascinated by ants creating a hill, or when I was digging in the dirt and watching the earthworms wiggle around to get into a darker, cooler place.

I loved playing, digging and feeling the cold, fertile world below my fingers. I was passionate about touching the earth and being a part of it.

Clearly, I was intrigued with the natural world. Those creatures were my little friends; I felt deeply connected to them. It was as if I were on an exploration of life in many forms as that little girl. Chasing butterflies, catching them in the net and then letting them go free was a favorite pastime. I was mesmerized when I watched the caterpillars crawling in the yard, And every summer, I was intrigued as I watched the fireflies sparkle as night descended.

I miss my kitty Cali; she was my best friend. She came to us as a surprise in our backyard, she and her two brothers were born there. We rescued them from the dangers of being feral after one of the babies was killed by a raccoon.

How was she able to steal my heart? She was a love that filled me that I didn't know was missing. It wasn't as if I hadn't had amazing cats and dogs live with me over the past 68 years. Something about Cali was different.

Call her a soul mate, call her just a pet who filled my heart, I don't know, I can't explain it; she was my heart. I still feel aglow when I look at her pictures or watch and listen to a video, as she sang with glee begging for her beloved treats.

When I was two years old, my Papa, my maternal grandfather who took me everywhere, took me to the circus in the big tent. He was strong and handsome and always made me feel loved and protected.

He bought me a painted turtle in a big oval glass bowl. I was so happy to have my little friend. Then one morning my turtle was not in his bowl. Mommy and I looked all over the apartment, behind the refrigerator, in the cabinets, under the furniture. We couldn't find my little friend. Of course, he must have died, and my parents told me he had escaped, probably to avoid the possibility that he had died. All I knew was that I never saw him again.

My parents bought me a canary when I was about six years old. He was the most beautiful little yellow bird who had the most glorious song you can imagine. I fed him and put the cover on his cage every night and uncovered him in the morning. He lived down in the kitchen in his little cage. We were best little friends, my Sweetie Pie and me.

When I practiced piano, not my favorite thing to do, he sang like there was no tomorrow. His voice was stunningly beautiful, a voice from bird land or the heavens. It was the most natural thing for him. As I played *Fur Elise* (Beethoven) or the *Spinning Song* (Albert Ellmenreich), he made my music sound like I was a famous pianist, because our duets brought me into a magical kingdom. Each evening he transported us to a world filled with beauty and love.

One morning I went to take the cover off his cage, and he was dead. I screamed and screamed, he had not been ill at all, and he had been serenading my parents and their friends the whole night prior to his demise. My sweet boy was gone. I was devastated.

Playing the piano has never been the same.

I always knew my pets would not live long. It's the love and companionship that makes it all worthwhile. My pets rescued me from my loneliness and emptiness, and I cared and loved them as my children.

When I was in seventh grade, we adopted the cutest, sweetest, gray-haired poodle. I was so thrilled. For some reason my parents wanted Pepe to sleep in a crate in the basement. That was the craziest idea because the poor little boy cried and howled and kept my parents awake. So, dad, always trying to be the savior, stayed in the basement with him. Pepe just wouldn't sleep in the crate, so dad was exhausted and not happy.

Finally, after a bunch of bad nights, maybe it was even a week, I begged my dad to let him sleep with me. I promised that he would sleep through the night with me in my bed and yup I was right, he slept with me every night until I went to college. Whenever I came home for a visit there he was by my side. It was tough on the little guy when I left to grow up and individuate from my parents. If I could have,

I would have taken him with me, but people didn't do that kind of thing in 1972.

Garcia was my hippy cool dude terrier mutt, named after Jerry. When I went to class he waited on the Syracuse University quad for me, then he accompanied me wherever I went. Everyone loved Garcia, even Pepe.

When I was living in Manhattan, working, and dating, the guy's attitude toward Garcia was a litmus test for whether I would see him again. My husband didn't skip a beat with Garcia. When my son was born, Garcia would sleep beside the playpen, protecting the little guy. He was such a spirited soul.

When I was not able to have more children, I filled the house with dogs and cats. I was not a crazy cat lady, but I was able to understand why there are crazy cat ladies. Our wonderful Karma, our gorgeous black cat who lived for over 21 years; Brandy, our stunning Golden who thought she was my daughter; Magic, our magnificent Persian who waited each night near the bottom of the steps and screamed for "Mom." Coco, the sweetest Golden in the world. Cali, the light of my life and Blackjack, the light of Josh's heart. Tabby and Princess, our outdoor feral cats for 14 years. Spots, our singing sweet kitty and Ollie, our awkward gorgeous kitty are still with us.

I filled the space where there was a huge hole. The love and companionship of my animals awakened my heart in ways that I never knew were possible.

We rescued each other.

10

DEATH

"Life is eternal; and love is immortal;
and death is only a horizon;
and a horizon is nothing save the limit of our sight."

~Rossiter Worthington Raymond

We sat on the floor of her very large walk-in closet in Boca Raton, Florida. A lifetime of jewelry sprawled on the floor. Piece by piece, they were memories of her life. The pearls from dad from their first anniversary. This was from here and that was from there. It was a bittersweet day.

She was given 18 months to live. The oncologist thought that the chemo she received for Hodgkin's Disease ten years prior caused her to develop AML, acute myeloid leukemia. There was no cure, she was 75. We were shocked and horrified. The thing that supposedly saved her life for 10 years ultimately killed her.

As my mother's life force was dissipating, the "I" I had been and grown into for 50 years was dissolving and reconfiguring; my pseudo foundation was shifting. Grief, loss, death, impermanence, shifting sands, heartbreak, sorrow.

Two days before my mother died, I heard a beautiful celestial chorus that sounded like sirens and harps welcoming her. I had been around quite a bit of death before but never had heard the chorus before, so I called Jason Shulman, my spiritual teacher, who knew a lot about death. "Yes," he said, "there is a chorus."
I too am dying.
Entering life, I breathed. And,
I began to die.
I am dying.
I don't know when, and I don't know how.
When I was 7, my mother's aunt died. We drove to the Bronx, somewhere near the Grand Concourse where most of my maternal grandmother's family lived. It was not a long ride, about an hour. I always loved looking out the window as we drove toward the family gatherings. There was something filled with light in those moments; love filled my pores.
The smells of brisket, chicken soup, and roasted chicken swirled through my little body as we entered the apartment building. Inside, the adults were sitting in a circle in the sunken living room, sullen and talking in Yiddish. The sound of the ancestors soothed me. There was lots of food, much sadness, and love.
I am dying.
I don't know where I will be,
Or who will be with me.
Or if I will be alone.
I forget, I remember,
I run, I return,
I am dying, time is precious.
I forget, I remember,
Life is precious.
I run, I return,

My body is sacred.

I forget, I remember, Life is short.

I live as if I can recover. I forget that I am dying. I fill up the spaces.

I was with a client who was dying. Beyond the precipice, the light was a bright, magnetic, golden orange. He had been diagnosed with pancreatic cancer one year following the traumatic and untimely death of his son. Our last several sessions were at his bedside.

In the healing, I saw him walking toward the precipice with a young boy. I sensed that I was not allowed to go too close to this magnificent light even though I was being magnetically drawn to it. I consciously pulled myself back, because I knew in my heart of hearts that it was not my time, that this transition was for my client. He fell asleep; 4 days later he passed.

I am dying.

I want my life to have meaning,

To live in alignment with my heart and the truth.

I have put death in another room, it is over there somewhere.

Not in this room,

Over there,

Far, far away.

Even though I have always yearned to connect with and embody my truest nature, I have made death a separate thing: there is life and then there is death.

Of course, I was brought up this way, children did not go to funerals or go to the cemetery. There is a separation that I created to feel safe a long time ago.

Jason Shulman has taught, *"death makes life and life makes death."* When I breathe this in, there is a sense of fresh air, like walking along the ocean's edge.

Iris was my dear friend, a soul sister — we met each other at the Gestalt Center of Long Island. She was a real renegade, a brilliant therapist, and a storyteller. She was terribly unhealthy, and all the psychotherapy she engaged with, as well as the medical interventions, did not save her. Iris underwent radical surgery, and was promised the sun, the moon, and the stars. I was upset that she chose to go in that direction. I knew, I just knew, that she wouldn't make it.

After the surgery, she went into a coma. We communicated with each other soul to soul telepathically that week and I started to feel the need to see her; she was at a Manhattan hospital.

Dressed in a gown for a black-tie affair, I visited her. When I arrived, she was in the final stages of dying; the nurse said she had about 12 hours left.

As I laid my hands on her and gave her a healing, we communicated. She did not want to leave; I told her that I did not want her to leave. I cried. She died 15 minutes later with my hands on her. I loved her deeply.

Deathing, Awakening,

My path, My true purpose unfolding.

Death of loved ones has brought me to a place where I could not be the same any longer. I became more aligned with Reality and the Intimate One. This has been a liberating path that had much suffering embedded in it. Maybe that's just how life is, maybe we should name it something else such as life/death or as it is, or the heart of the matter. I don't know but separating it all doesn't work.

Dying, Awakening,

To this world and to this life As It Is.

Maybe what is important, is that healing is about having moments that are enlightening and awakening and not that we have to attain anything at the end of the search. Maybe it is just about being our best selves.

My path includes being mother, grandmother, wife, healer, teacher, friend, sister, and daughter.

I am not who I was nor am I who I thought I would be. I am certainly not who I was raised to be.

Through all the difficulties that have unfolded in my life, and there were many, I wanted to fight and fix what was happening. I have realized that I have to allow each moment to be itself.

Awakening, enlightening, birthing, deathing.

Primal sounds.

No familiar landmarks.

Few known locations.

Uncertainty abounds.

Places of non-definition.

"I" disintegrating.

I AM Becoming.

Inside/Outside,

Impermanence,

Dancing.

On October 2, 2007, as my father lay in the hospice bed, Jamie, my husband, and I sat by his side, as his breathing was changing. I sensed more changing than his breath. I felt this feeling of the father whom I had known prior to his cognitive loss. It was remarkable because this feeling of more wholeness was happening as he literally was leaving his body. I turned to Jamie and asked him if he sensed the shift. He said he felt it as well. There was also this larger-than-life feeling in the room along with us. I knew we were not alone.

Larry Marder was more present than he had been for years or maybe ever in his life. Psychically, he showed me many of the homes he lived in, and he was changing his home again, he was leaving the home that we had had together in this life. As he took his final breath, he was a seed blossoming.

After my father died, I went through a period of many months where I was very internal in a way I had never been before.

I used to take a step into the world without thinking, without really being present — yes, even with all the therapy and spiritual practice and healing work I had engaged with. Now I was ready to walk through the gate of the garden where my true self had been waiting.

Death and awakening have birthed me an internal mother and father, who have allowed me to move in my natural rhythm most of the time. I touched liberation as I crawled out of that dark poisonous cave and was rebirthed into the world. Death has called to me, waking me up.

Awakening,

Things that I thought were—are not,

My story disappeared.

Life is not eternal,

Something of which we are part of is eternal.

Different Eyes, Different Ears, New Blood, Dying, Awakening.

Now I know; I am a midwife to life and into death. Grief along with love brings a depth of healing that knows no bounds.

11

HATRED

"When we are no longer able to change a situation,
we are challenged to change ourselves."

~Viktor E. Frankl

Hatred.
I hate and you hate. We all hate.

The Montagues and the Capulets, the Hatfields and the McCoys, Alexander Hamilton and Aaron Burr, Esau and Jacob.

Loathing, abhorring, ill will, disgust, resentment, animosity, and hostility toward another.

It is a human phenomenon.

The problem is, we don't know how to deal with hate. Hatred arises from racial, religious, sexual identity differences, and insecurity. It is often a real reaction to wrongdoing, betrayal, abuse, having been disrespected, dehumanized, objectified, or manipulated. We don't respect individual differences.

We could have been educated to hate as part of a family or group culture.

So many paths lead to hatred.

Stop hatred now! It's not enough to say that. That just isn't the way.

The fact that we have hateful thoughts and feelings isn't the problem.

The problem is that hatred is dangerous. It is dangerous when it is acted out in some way. Either outward onto others or inward toward ourselves.

It's not that we have thoughts that are filled with hatred; it's what we do and don't do with them. The thing is, we all have hateful, unevolved thoughts and feelings for all sorts of reasons.

As a child, my father read accounts of the Holocaust to us during the holidays. Mostly, I was confused. Emotions were muddled up in my heart. I believe that the basic thing I felt was fear — fear about being Jewish.

I didn't know how to process what I learned so I began reading every book I could get my hands on. There weren't very many in the 1960's.

When I read the book *Night* by Elie Wiesel, a Holocaust survivor, writer, professor, and political activist, I could hear, feel, and smell the events he described. I took Elie's experiences of starvation, and torture into my being. I vowed to make a difference in the world.

Early on, I thought that the problem with the world was that there was a small fraternity of evil doers and we, the innocent good ones, had to do everything we could to win against them. They were the perpetrators, and I aligned with the victims.

Little did I know, I needed to heal my own personal suffering to be a deeply authentic, compassionate, healing presence.

It was September of 1979, Jamie and I were on our honeymoon in Puerto Vallarta, Mexico. We decided to go on an excursion to learn about the history of the area. There was another young couple on the outing with us. We had not met them before.

Part of the tour was to take us, the American tourists, to an outdoor restaurant where we were served the local fare. We also went to a home where Elizabeth Taylor and Richard Burton had lived and of course made a stop or two at a Mexican gift shop selling handmade folklore objects.

When we got back into the van, the young woman said to her husband, *"Did you Jew them down?"* I was horrified.

My youth was sheltered and filled with people who were either Jewish or Catholic. I rarely experienced antisemitism. As I matured, I became more aware of it. I could feel the hatred in my bones if someone hated me just because I was a Jew even when it was outwardly hidden. The hatred seeped through the ethers and being a sensitive person, I knew it and picked it up.

Over the years, I realized that I couldn't control other people's hatred toward me whether it was antisemitism or something else. And as a psychotherapist and healer, I realized that I had to take a deep look at myself and own my hatred in order to be a true healing and compassionate presence.

The big awakening was that I didn't want to know I had hatred inside of me. It was taboo and it would mean that I was bad. So, it remained hidden, and I acted it out.

As a young child I developed survival mechanisms to not be in touch with all of my aliveness and all of who I was. I carried many false beliefs about myself. I protected myself this way; after all, it was better than having others think my character was flawed or even worse, that I was a heartless person.

I believed I should be a certain way to be loved. Any powerful and seemingly negative behavior was thwarted by turning it against myself.

As a teenager, I was a part of the "in crowd." I was popular enough, a good athlete, smart enough, and above all, I was safe. But I didn't know how to deal with my emotions. Simultaneously, I had developed a judgmental streak. There was a girl at camp and a few of us weren't inclusive toward her. I never said anything cruel directly to her, but if my energy was felt, it was hateful, I am sure of it. I felt powerful and significant. Fifty years later, we were both at a camp reunion, I went up to her and we had a short, good discussion.

Another way I hid my own hatred toward others was I held onto the belief that everyone had a good heart at their core. I didn't want to acknowledge when danger was looking at me in the face, it just felt safer. Of course, I now know, it wasn't safer. My hatred had to be hidden and repressed.

What I realized through years of engaging in consciousness-raising activities was that I had a small but often very loud voice inside my head that was critical, judgmental, and hateful toward myself. I became immune to it; it was just something I needed to live with.

I tried to fit into an image of how I thought I should be and not be who I was. It worked out pretty well until I realized that I wanted more realness in my life. I needed to face myself — all of me.

But there was that nagging voice there: you should be this way or you are this or that. I avoided and dismissed myself a lot.

As I paid attention to my thinking, it was sort of like watching a movie, but I was the movie. It was so helpful and healing and awakening, as my wise-self guided me to realize that my self-hatred was the avoidance of my suffering, vulnerability, fragility, fears, insecurity, and power.

Self-hatred was clearly a creative way to protect myself. I was the victim and the perpetrator all wrapped up in one tightly held package. I really suffered from this a great deal.

I sheltered myself from the storm that may have prevailed if I had been in touch with and expressed the truth more often.

I clung to self-protection and withdrew myself into myself. This part of me was resigned to being unhappy and hidden.

The hater was victorious, I conquered and dominated myself all the time. The truth is, suppressing self-hatred is toxic. It helps us avoid reality when we don't want to be in relationship with the truth about our lives. Allowing reality in even though it is difficult to do at times, helps us to grow into more compassionate humans. When I realized this, my life changed!!

My truest nature blossomed and opened.

I became much more tolerant of my own suffering. I was able to be present to myself day and night. I was more real, authentic, and honest.

Whenever I feel judgmental, I own it and bring it into my heart. I know I am protecting something, and I say *"Hello, welcome home!"*

The truth of my hatred, my pain and suffering, brought more aliveness and light into my body-mind-spirit. I went from being constricted to creative self-expression.

Sometimes, I still hear that cruel voice; I acknowledge it and sometimes I laugh and have a good talk with it. We have a real relationship now.

Inner conflicts were safer than outer conflicts, so I had to do a lot of learning about how to be in conflict. I remember when I was first learning how to do this, I would put my hand on my heart and talk from my heart. It was remarkable, I could slow down and breathe and feel more of myself and be truly honest even if I was shaking internally. Standing up and facing conflict has been so freeing. I needed to feel safe internally to deal with the conflicts of life.

I no longer leave myself out. I am more compassionate and freer.

Realizing the truth of what I did to myself didn't kill me; it freed me. Honestly, I still feel hatred toward others sometimes, but I don't act it out. I feel it, I go to the root of it, I wrestle with it. It's a process and I am not hurting myself or others.

Giving it a place in my heart allows it to transform instead of getting rid of it where it infects all of me.

Healing self-hatred is not about trying to force ourselves to be positive or reframing our negative thoughts. I believe we must develop a relationship with those thoughts and see what arises from that.

Give your hatred a home in your heart.

12

DRUGS, SEX,
ROCK & ROLL, AND GURUS

"Nothing behind me,
everything ahead of me, as is ever so on the road."

~Jack Kerouac

I was a counselor-in-training at a sleep-away camp in the Catskill Mountains of New York. It was the summer of *Woodstock*. I wanted to go the concert, but I was a bit too young, so I experimented with marijuana for the first time. There was a vibrancy I had never known, the dirt road, the trees, the lake, the sky, my hands, everything was alive and shimmering. I felt held in a larger wholeness, it was thrilling.

After a while, marijuana was not my go-to in order to be more in touch with reality and freedom. It was 1970, the time of free love, and the counterculture was in full swing. I attended rallies against the Vietnam War, I rejected any conservative viewpoint, anything that was a societal norm, and inequality on any level.

My heart's desire was to save the world. Even though my parents supported my anti-establishment beliefs, I left their home in the summer of 1972 and migrated to upstate New York to study at Syracuse University.

Not only was I longing for freedom in every sense of the word, but I needed to individuate from my parents and create a new life. Even though I was passionate about my studies, my truest longing was for personal, political, emotional, and spiritual enlightenment.

Fast forward to college. A group of us gravitated toward each other until we had a constant group of about 10 of us. We communed together, explored together, studied together, and ate together. We were kindred spirits.

Our promise was to explore reality, life, and become free together. Psychedelic trips, sex, and rock and roll were at the top of the list. Psilocybin-magic mushrooms, mescaline-orange sunshine, LSD, and MDMA.

Contrary to a lot of what was the societal view of what psychedelic trips did to people, these experiences changed my perspective of life for the better. For me, they were a direct portal to the real and the multi-dimensions that are always present.

Gratefully, these direct drug-induced experiences of altered states of reality were awesome. I gained clarity about life, I saw the shimmering of space, colors were musical, and I could see music as it traveled through space.

My time was filled with philosophical discussions, political rallies, hippie poetry and the exploration of reality. If an activity, movie, or book wasn't a part of the counterculture, I wasn't interested. I identified as part of the wheat germ, yogurt, granola, vegetarian, earth shoes, flower-power, cool and hip generation.

Many of my inspirational guides were found in books; Kerouac's *On the Road* and *Dharma Bums*, Ken Kesey,

Timothy Leary, Gary Snyder, Richard Brautigan, Yogananda, Black Elk and Castaneda. The cult favorites on campus were books by Robert Heinlein, Kurt Vonnegut, and of course Herman Hesse.

They knew me and I knew them. And I longed for more.

I was hooked and freeing the bonds of my history. *Our Bodies Ourselves, Women and Madness, MS Magazine, Fear of Flying,* all inducted me into feminism and spirituality in a new way.

They knew me and I knew them. And I longed for more.

Janis Joplin, Gracie, Joan Baez, Janis Ian, Carol King, Laura Nyro — oh my goodness what women!! I could count on them. Their music caressed me and made me proud to be a woman.

They knew me and I knew them. And I longed for more.

The Grateful Dead, Allman Brothers, Jessie Colin Young, Dylan, James Taylor, I loved, loved, loved them and they helped me know that I was part of something beautiful and grand. And we were changing the world.

They knew me and I knew them. And I longed for more.

That first year of college when I was getting high, I was also freely having sex mostly with one guy. It helped me to feel alive, vital, and not alone. Sex was paired with drugs and some cigarette smoking. Sadly, I didn't respect my body, it was a tool to help me feel my aliveness.

Even though I was sexually free, I was usually monogamous. I wanted to experience the high and ecstasy of sex and was selective with the guys I dated but not aware. I was not looking for it to be a spiritual experience, I was only concerned with freedom.

But then a friend of mine in my freshman dorm got venereal crabs and we all freaked out. There was a lot to learn and being careful had not been a top priority for me.

All of this said, the freedom of sexual expression was important to me, but my fundamental desire was to heal and become a liberated woman. I attempted to challenge the traditional beliefs regarding sexuality. It was empowering to choose when to have sex and when not to. And I was very lucky.

The drug journeys confirmed for me that there was so much more to life than the sheltered world in which I had grown up. The doors of perception flew wide open, and I checked in.

I surrendered. I received answers to the many questions I wrestled with, even though I often forgot the specifics the next day when I was in my everyday young adult college persona. I was more whole and broke through an inner barrier that had held me captive and hidden.

There was a lot more I needed to do to reach the state where I could integrate the wisdom that I touched, felt, perceived, and heard. It was all in my heart.

I trusted these people in a way I never had trusted a group of friends in the past. I didn't love everyone in our little group, but I adored the heart and soul of each person.

They knew me and I knew them. And I longed for more.

The Big Chill (a 1983 movie) was us, with all the music of the times, the confused relationships, and a sad tragic suicide of one of the most wonderful, loving, lonely, and brilliant guys I have known. I still miss you, Barry.

One of our friends discovered yoga. He invited us to a meeting in one of the lecture halls at the university to see a video of the guru from India who was living, practicing, and teaching in Pennsylvania. I was entranced.

Honestly, I thought that having a guru would save me; after all, the Beatles had gone to India and met with the Maharishi Mahesh Yogi and they had only positive experiences. And, Ram Dass, previously known as Richard Alpert, who was experimenting with Timothy Leary at Harvard

University as professors, was devoted to his guru from India, Neem Karoli Baba. And I respected them. I could sense there was something to these gurus that I had never before known.

So, I thought that maybe this Indian guru living right here on the East Coast would magically teach me how be open-hearted, positive, and happy all the time. I wanted to be able to rise above the difficulties of life.

I joined a small yoga group connected to the ashram that met at 5:00 a.m. each morning. I don't know how I did that. We practiced asanas, jogged around Thorndon Park, meditated, and chanted. Maybe, just maybe, I had found Shangri-La ... but danger was lurking.

I wanted to chant *Om Shanti*, One Peace, all day, and all night. I was looking for that oneness to lose myself in and I erroneously thought at the time, that was how I would be my true self. I believed that getting away from the difficulties, suffering, and reality of life and the world was the goal and that merging with the Oneself of reality and leaving behind everything else was the answer.

I longed to have access to the hidden unseen worlds to receive healing and transformation somehow. I wanted to merge with the light and not know about the darkness and the suffering that was inside of me.

The first time I arrived at the ashram, everyone was dressed in white yoga clothing and milling about. The campus was simultaneously beautiful and a little creepy. Are all these people the walking dead in their outfits that make them look like angels? But I didn't pay attention to my inner voice.

What would happen here? Well, it certainly took me on a journey through many places I would not have experienced without going there.

The guru was a tall, handsome, dark-skinned man. I was at the front door putting my shoes on the shelf, I turned around and there he was. I was breathless, I stood still as he was escorted into an auditorium. I was awe-struck.

At the front of the room was a small, raised platform with flowers, a huge picture of his guru, Babaji, whose picture transmitted love. Everyone stood up as the guru entered the room, they all hit the floor and bowed, followed by saying some sort of chant or prayer. Then there was chanting and ecstatic movements and sounds as the guru sat down and played his harmonium. I didn't know if I belonged, but I stayed.

Being confronted with bowing brought up anxiety and inner questioning. In Judaism, we don't make idols before us, there is only the One. How could I bow to a guru? Will that mean I will be punished? Will I have an awakening from bowing? Those were all legitimate questions that I needed to explore and live with.

More importantly, I sensed that something was wrong. A dear boyfriend who I adored had moved there so I decided to push myself. I went against what I was feeling.

After many trips down to the ashram I filled out the application to be initiated, but then I held the paper. I froze and immediately threw it in the garbage. My mind thought it was time to take the next step, but my heart kept saying "no!" Slowly, I started to pay attention to myself, and it wasn't easy to follow what was inside my heart and what I perceived.

In retrospect, I realized that this guru was transmitting seduction, not healing!

There has been a great deal of sexual misconduct amongst gurus who came to the United States. Some were charged and found guilty, some were never charged; there are many articles and documentaries on this subject.

I am grateful that my young self knew to leave even though it was so enticing. I am happy to say that there are spiritual teachers who are safe, honest, ethical, and wise.

13

RESISTANCE

"Stay with it, there is a jewel inside."

Resistance, blockages, opposition, obstacles! For many years the appearance of any sort of personal resistance had been a roadblock for me. It kept showing its face and getting in my way, or that's what I thought.

When I have been blocked in any way it felt like I was in opposition to myself, what I wanted to accomplish, say, or be. I tried all kinds of ways to rid myself of that "evil" resistance. I pushed through, I avoided, I ignored it, and then I would push some more.

I believed I shouldn't resist in any form, ever. My thinking went something like this: I should be open and flowing whenever I thought and decided it was time to flow. I was focused on progress, and I was attainment oriented. I clearly wasn't in relationship with all of myself, though.

The flow state is so pleasurable. I'm productive, creative, expressing myself and free. There is an ease to it. I feel connected and engaged with my life force, whether it is the feeling of the creative force working through me and into my knitting needles, or into an essay, or exercising, or baking a new recipe. I am in sync and relaxed. I want to go on and on until I need to rest. And then, the rest is well-earned.

And then there is the state of resistance, where my flow appears to have abandoned me. At these times, I have experienced an internal war zone. I have judged myself harshly, which only makes it all worse.

It was as if I believed there was an on/off switch that I could command to be turned on when the time was right. It seemed, however, that I was trying to fit square pegs into round holes.

I couldn't allow the resistance to be what it was. Subsequently, I was not able to receive any of the wisdom, it was all about the fight. I wasn't allowing the natural ebb and flow of life.

There used to be a popular Chinese handcuffs toy where you would put the cylinder of paper onto a finger on one hand and then on the other hand and pull in the opposite direction. Then it would get tighter, and you couldn't take it off.

The trick was that pulling in a direction that we thought something should go in is the most incorrect thing to do. By relaxing the fingers, we could easily slip the paper contraption off.

I kept resistance separate from me, I didn't want to relate to it or accept it as a part of me. It was my enemy and I only wanted friends. I did not want to tolerate resistance in any way.

I attempted to experience only what I wanted. It was as if I didn't have enough peripheral vision. My eyes and focus were ahead of me and in the future.

I kept resistance at arm's length, was not tolerant of its force, and I was unwilling to receive its wisdom. Was I foolish!!

After years of fighting against what I perceived was resistance, I realized that something important was going on and I wasn't paying attention. For the longest time, I didn't consider the fact that there is a natural unfolding of life and that I couldn't push the river no matter what, period.

Maybe I need to respect it, listen to it, and give it a place to live. And maybe just maybe, there were seeds of something life-enhancing within it.

After years of misunderstanding, I began to explore what resistance really was saying to me. What was its message?

Maybe resistance is good. After all, if our body is resistant to certain viruses, bacteria, or diseases, that can be the foundation for health.

Maybe I am refusing to accept something, maybe it is a place of rest or transition.

I realized that resistance can be incredibly beneficial on every level. I wish I had realized that sooner.

Sometimes being resistant means standing up to something that I feel is wrong — like being a resistance fighter. The underground, secret resistance groups that sprang up across Europe to oppose the Nazi's during World War II made a significant difference for the Allies. Despite danger, these groups of people clandestinely met and created networks of resistance against the German attempts to reign supreme.

Maybe it's going against the status quo.

Maybe it's many other things and just not the sensate feeling I prefer.

Pausing, changing direction, time for nourishment, space for contemplation, opening the gate into more light, more consciousness and more of my true nature.

Maybe there is a lot of preparation happening; maybe in the restful stage I am gestating and preparing for the flow. Maybe I am incubating, and recalibrating.

As I held my resistance close to my heart and allowed it to touch me and not keep it separate, I realized that my resistance was the medicine I needed. There was wisdom in the resistance; I just needed to get to the place where I could bear it and be in relationship with it.

I needed to be where I was. I needed to be open to the state of consciousness that was not in flow and hear, sense, perceive, and realize there is information and wisdom in the resistance.

As I developed a real relationship with resistance, I began to open my eyes and receive messages about what I needed. Sometimes I just needed a break, sometimes I needed to reconsider what and where I was headed and sometimes, I needed to live with the state of pause and allow the gestation of my projects to grow — and not force a pre-mature birth.

As I developed the muscle to be where I was and with whatever showed up, I was more relaxed and more open, not necessarily ready to finish a project but more open to the wisdom of the moment.

Everything has its own rhythm. Sometimes I must start over, sometimes I need time and space. And sometimes I need to embrace the unknown and uncertainty.

When held consciously, resistance can be a gateway. A gateway to creativity and flow, a gateway to more embodiment, an opening that is closed, it calls our attention to it, it is trying to tell us something, there is information stored in there.

14

INTUITION

"I believe in intuitions and inspirations... I sometimes
FEEL that I am right. I do not KNOW that I am."

~Albert Einstein

Sunday mornings, Jericho, New York, the late 1950's.
Somehow, don't ask me how, I often knew things. Dad
had a Sunday-morning ritual. He sat on the large blue
chair beside the table with the sculptured lamp, his pipe
emitting the soothing aroma of cherry tobacco. The *New
York Times* was sprawled out on the ottoman as he read the
sports and the stock pages.

One day dad showed me the stock page and asked me
which one I thought he should buy. Well, it wasn't a thought.
As I sat on his lap, the name Xerox showed itself to me, it
emblazoned itself on the page.

And of course, you can imagine that dad made money
on that investment. So, we did that on various Sundays, I
was daddy's lucky little girl.

Intuition is our natural instinctual knowing. It arises in
us as a thought, an image, a "gut" feeling or just a knowing.

My father often told me that "children are to be seen and not heard." I found it very confusing because I always knew when things just weren't right, I could feel it in my whole body. But I got the message, and I learned to resign myself to not inquiring about certain things. I was conflicted.

I developed a hypervigilant ability — an elevated sense of knowing when I was safe. I was on high alert. Through my preteen years I learned how to keep quiet and keep things to myself. I often didn't allow myself to know about difficult circumstances. I received information and ignored it for a very long time.

And yet my intuition was still active, very much alive. I just blocked the negative things from touching my heart. I always knew when something was amiss, I could feel it in every fiber of my being.

When I took exams, I could often see the answer on the exact page in the textbook where I had read about the subject. It was as if my consciousness brought me to a different land when I was under pressure and some part of me would get the book I had studied from and illuminate the paragraph where the answer was. It was remarkable.

But I had to study for that to happen. I took it for granted when I had those experiences, because I had them for most of my life. I didn't know about the mind-body-spirit connection at all, it was just something that happened to me, and I didn't question it.

It was the summer of 1977; I was writing my master's thesis at Syracuse University. As I walked into the Marine Midland Bank, I heard me saying to myself, "If I wasn't crazy, I would think that those two boys just robbed the bank." Well guess what, I wasn't crazy, and I didn't even know that I had thought I was crazy until that moment.

I walked into the bank as the two armed-robbers walked out. The doors locked behind me; it was scary. All of us who were witnesses to the robbery in some way spent quite a bit of time together that summer, we weren't allowed to leave Syracuse until the case was closed. Even though I was too terrified to point out one of the robbers in the lineup, luckily, he was so terrified by the whole experience that he plead guilty.

Intuition was safe to use in some ways, but not when I felt danger in some way.

I wasn't aware that I didn't trust myself until that event. This woke me up and I started to work on myself in a whole new way. Most importantly, I allowed myself to finally realize I was extremely intuitive.

I started to pay attention to my inner voice. As I listened to it, it became louder and took more of a prominent place inside me. I felt less threatened about sensing and knowing about negative things as well as those things that would help me. I wasn't willing to turn myself and my intuition off any longer. Sometimes it was helpful and sometimes it was devastating.

This even spilled into my romantic life when I intuitively knew I shouldn't go forward. I had just returned from two months in Europe, and I immediately flew to Chicago to see my college boyfriend. Suddenly, I had a vision and a deep knowing that I couldn't be with him because he would ultimately end up taking his life. I received the phone call in the winter of 2010, he had committed suicide.

I was on jury duty in downtown Manhattan in the early 80's. I was a juror on an armed robbery case and gave the defendant the benefit of the doubt. They should never have picked me to be on the jury. How crazy, I was a young mental-health professional. We were in the jury room, and I was the holdout. I just couldn't see the truth. I was being pressured to decide but couldn't make the decision. I went into the bathroom and locked the door. I started to cry, I was beside myself, I was afraid of putting somebody who was innocent in jail.

I was under tremendous pressure and prayed from my heart, "*Please, dear God, show me the truth.*" In an instant the whole truth about the robbery was revealed to me. I flushed the toilet, washed my hands, and went back in the room. I told the rest of the jurors that I agreed with them, he was guilty. A few months later I was walking to work, and I ran into the judge from the case. She asked me who the holdout was. "*Me,*" I said. I never saw her again.

The intensity of being the holdout and on a jury was so stressful. I felt danger and couldn't allow myself to be present enough to see the truth until I felt additional pressure from the other jurors. Thankfully, I was able to get to the truth. My fear of putting a young man in jail for a long time made me deaf, dumb, and blind until I was under pressure to decide.

Reclaiming our intuition is natural when we are willing to take responsibility for who we are, because reality rushes in.

One day during the summer of 1984, Josh and I were driving in Long Beach. He was a few months old. Suddenly, I felt magnetically pulled to stop in front of a house on a corner. I had a strong feeling it was the house where I spent the first summer of my life. The good news was that I listened to myself and checked it out.

There were no cell phones back then so when I arrived home, I called mom and she said, "*Yes, that was it.*" I was astounded and felt grounded inside of myself.

I needed validation for all these seemingly strange events. I needed to know that I was not crazy. It was a relief for me to feel more relaxed in who I was.

Being intuitive was not something that was discussed back in the '50s and '60s. People started to open more to these innate abilities in the '70s and '80s.

A few years later, we were at the beach; I was taking a nap and felt an earthquake was coming. I could feel the earth moving and I heard some sounds. I checked the news when we arrived home. I was accurate but the earthquake was in California, and we were on Long Island, New York. How in the world could that happen? That was the beginning of allowing myself to know how everything really is interconnected.

As I started to trust myself more and as I matured, I became more open to knowing about painful and difficult things. As I healed and developed myself on personal and spiritual levels my intuition became more of an ordinary knowing about everyday occurrences, not just extreme events.

It was the summer of 2001; we were going on a family trip to Israel. There had been a lot of unrest in Israel. Several of my psychotherapy clients were very upset that I was going. I simply said, "Well you know, there could be a terrorist attack right here." They probably thought I was just in denial.

Two nights prior to the 9/11 attacks on the United States, I had a dream where there was fire and a lot of smoke, I jumped out of bed onto the floor and took cover like when we used to do air-raid drills in the late 1950s and early 1960s. The horror of 9/11 happened in my city as well as in Pennsylvania and in Washington, D.C.

Healing work, psychotherapy, spiritual practices, expressing my creativity, have all been ways I have developed myself and awakened a natural ability to be intuitive.

Cultivating my intuition deepened as I healed my childhood traumas. It was not about becoming psychic; it was about being who I am.

At first, I played guessing games with myself: who's calling, will I find a parking spot, which highway should I take?

It helped me to develop the muscle of intuition. The more I listened and trusted myself, the safer I felt and the more I was in touch with what was happening in the moment. It has been a real departure from being hypervigilant and having to go outside of myself to attempt to know what I was around to feel safe.

At this point, I listen to my intuition most of the time. And when I push something away that seems irrational, I always say the same thing: *why didn't I listen!!* At this point I laugh at myself or slap my head lightly like that cute emoji. Like really, of course I should have listened.

15

RITUAL

"In the name of ritual, we can do anything.
We can do astonishing acts."

~Barbara Myerhoff

R ituals have been a conscious way for me to mark passages, whether it was a celebration of some sort such as birthdays, weddings, graduations, bris milah, baby naming's or holidays and for times of death and loss. Some of them are religiously based such as sitting shiva after a death or the gathering with family and reading the Haggadah each Passover to honor the memory of the journey of the Jewish people from slavery into freedom.

Personally, I have created daily rituals as a spiritual practice. They have been and are a portal into my connection with life. They support me in honoring where I am and who I am along with embracing the mundane, my joys, and my sorrows.

Rituals help me to connect to the sacredness of life as I sink into gratitude for each moment. I remember how precious it is that I have been blessed to awaken to another day.

I don't look for meaning through these rituals as much as I look to connect to myself, my loved ones, and life itself. The truth is, as I bring and cultivate more presence within myself, I have more capacity to be a healing presence for all that life brings.

Each morning, my rituals look something like this: wash up, put essential oils on, some type of exercise, prayer, and meditation. This supports my heart, my mind, my body, and my soul on all levels. It helps me to create my intention for healing that day.

Since I am flexible, my rituals are not always in the same order. I just flow into what feels right as the next thing to do. On most Saturdays, I meander about, and the rituals are done slowly throughout the morning and early afternoon.

A few hours later, I engage in a tea ritual.

I have been drinking tea since I was a young girl, I will always remember that orange red box of *Sweet Touch Nee Tea*, which is a combo of black teas from India, Java, and Ceylon. It was delicious then and it warmed me. We drank tea in the morning and after dinner and it was always on a holiday table. I didn't like coffee, even though I tried to. I guess all the tea drinking early on was about so many things, but I loved the aroma. It soothed my soul no matter what was going on in my little world.

Slowly, I fill the tea pot with filtered water. Carefully, I warm the water. Depending on what type of tea I am brewing I choose a different temperature. If it's green tea the temperature needs to be lower than white, red, or black tea, so I have a tea pot that calculates the exact temperature. Not too hot and not too cold, it's just right.

As the water is warming, I choose the tea. Usually, I start with green jasmine pearls. I count out a small number of pearls and put them inside an unbleached tea sac. Then

I choose the mug; some days it is insulated glass and other days it is a handmade object from my travels.

Once the water has warmed, I carefully pour it on top of the tea sac and time the brewing for 3 to 4 minutes, depending on how strong I want the tea that morning. If it is too bitter and has steeped for too long, I spill out the tea and start anew.

Then I decide where I will sit as I sip the tea. In the winter, I sit either next to the window in the kitchen and gaze at the trees in the yard or in the living room near the fireplace. In warmer weather, I go outdoors.

Holding the mug in my hands warms me. I appreciate the warmth anytime of the year. It's so soothing and healing. As I am warmed on the inside, I also become aware of the outside of me.

With my first sip of tea, my mouth comes alive with all sorts of sensations. When I smell the aroma, the synapses in my brain fire and wake up. I am present and even more centered in myself.

I gaze outside. I take in the moment and breathe. I have thoughts about the day ahead and then return to my tea, taking in the air around me, the sounds, my kitties, and my husband if he is around.

As I continue sipping my tea, I am transported somewhere in the world where the tea was grown and harvested. Perhaps it was in China, India, Tibet, or England. I feel a deep connection with the tea growers, the earth, the plants, the trees, and the atmosphere of the plantation.

Miraculously, when the seeds are sown and fed the right amount of water and sunlight and cared for properly, they grow into plants or trees where the tea leaves are harvested by hand and then made ready for market.

Gratitude and true, simple pleasure fill me. It's an enormous blessing that I can bring the world into my home, that

I have a home and that I am safe. I feel the mystery of life, never knowing what the next unfolding will be.

I can be with things as they are whether precious or disturbing, breath-by-breath and with each sip.

Returning to my daily rituals soothes my soul. On a deeper level, this heals the places in me that suffer from feeling separate. These rituals bring me to the interconnectedness of life.

These rituals carry me through the day as I touch the play of the world.

A remarkable thing about this is that I am clearly setting up conditions of healing myself and others through this practice. Since I drink tea throughout the day, each time I take a cup of tea to warm me up I feel the entire healing shape from earlier that day; it repeatedly brings me home to my heart and to the world.

In 2020, we sold our beautiful Manhattan apartment, it was my refuge. It took such good care of me for more than 10 years. We slept there each week, I gave healing sessions there and then when I taught my healing intensives, I was there alone in that sacred space. I loved being in Manhattan, it feels like home for me in a way that no other place does.

I didn't want to let it go. People reminded me that when one door closes another one opens; I believe that. But all rationale aside, my heart broke as we prepared it for viewing and the sale. Part of me believed that wherever else I lived, I would also live there forever.

Integrating rituals supported me with each step that I took in saying good-bye. I spoke to my apartment and thanked it as we prepared to leave. I promised that we would find someone else to love it as I had. And we did!

I donated many of the items to people in need. That felt good, and I wept as I gave each bit away. I was so attached to the safety of that sweet space.

The morning before the moving truck arrived, for the last time I thanked every tiny part of the apartment, the closets, the shelving, the floor, the windows, the amazing bathroom, and little kitchenette. I cried and with much difficulty I said good-bye once more and closed the door, leaving the keys on the kitchen counter.

16

SYNCHRONICITY

"Synchronicity is an ever-present reality
for those who have eyes to see."

~Carl G. Jung

C arl G. Jung, a famous Swiss psychiatrist, founded the field of analytical psychology. His influences were from the fields of psychology, anthropology, archaeology, literature, and philosophy. He is well known for his concepts of individuation, archetypes and the collective unconscious.

Jung believed that synchronicity was an unusual coincidence that could be meaningful. Yet, I don't think they are coincidences. I think what synchronicity points to is something much larger than what we obfuscate in our everyday lives most of the time. Perhaps the appearance of a synchronistic event opens us to the interconnections that exist in a larger paradigm of reality.

My mother was an artist, and I always loved art. We often went to art exhibits together, whether it was taking a trip down to Philadelphia and being immersed in the collection at the Barnes Foundation or seeing the newest exhibit at all the inspiring museums in Manhattan.

It was something mom and I could easily do together. There was so much discord between us in my teenage years, so it was wonderful to enter a world that we both loved together. Those trips were heart-opening, healing moments for us.

The MOMA, the Museum of Modern Art on 53rd Street in Manhattan, had a Picasso exhibit in 1980. Because it was such a popular exhibit, we had to buy tickets in advance and stand online outdoors as we awaited our time slot. There was nothing unusual at that point.

As we entered the museum we were directed to the correct gallery. I was always intrigued by Picasso's cubism; why were so many of his paintings like that? What was going on inside of him? He had survived living in a war-torn country as a child, how did that trauma with so much tragedy affect his art?

Shortly after we entered the exhibit, I suddenly turned around and realized that Mom and I were in a gallery with Jackie Onassis and a couple of Secret Service agents. I was shocked and thrilled; we walked through the whole exhibit together, we acknowledged each other but there was no talking and no interacting.

How did that happen? That would never be allowed in today's world. Was the fact that we were there at that moment with Jackie O a coincidence? What were the odds that these two women — Jackie O and my mom (who were born just hours apart) would be in the same exhibit? And more: that the Secret Service allowed mom and me to wander through the galleries with Jackie O? Unheard of!

Mom was born in New Haven, Connecticut, on July 27, 1929, and Jackie was born in Southampton, New York on July 28, 1929. They both were intelligent, talented, and beautiful women. Even though they were both college graduates and worked in their chosen artistic field, they lived very different lives.

Jackie was a socialite and former first lady of the United States until the tragic murder of her husband, President John F. Kennedy. Mom was a part-time professional woman who was immersed in the arts and lived more of a 1950-1960 suburban housewife lifestyle.

They both were diagnosed with Lymphoma at 63 years old; mom with Hodgkin's Lymphoma and Jackie with non-Hodgkin's Lymphoma. Jackie died a few months after she started chemotherapy. Mom lived until 2005 when she developed a type of leukemia that was caused by one of the chemotherapy drugs she had had ten years earlier.

Was our meeting a coincidence? It still would have been an amazing experience if Lauren Bacall or Liza Minelli walking through the exhibit with us, but the similarities in mom's and Jackie's lives, illnesses and deaths, well that's something else.

Synchronicity. There was this other-worldly feeling, as if we were catapulted into a sacred space together with art that we loved, with our love for each other, with our admiration of this incredible woman who had been first lady of the United States, who had suffered through horrific public tragedy, who was loved and adored by so many. It felt as if there was divine intervention. We felt blessed by her presence. Maybe she even felt blessed by ours.

The phenomenon of synchronicity brought me to realize the reality that something larger holds this whole life together like a beautiful, tattered weaving.

It was a snowy winter. Brandy, my beautiful golden retriever who mated and birthed three beautiful girls, went into the yard with her one-year-old daughter, Coco. They loved to play in the yard and "do their business there" throughout the day. Suddenly the doorbell rang, there was a woman who I had never seen before at the door. She said one of our goldens was hit by a car and in a serious way, the other she saw run home.

The gate to the backyard was open and we didn't realize it. The dogs got out of the yard and were running around the neighborhood when our sweetest girl was hit. These amazing people picked her up and took her to the emergency 24-hour care veterinary hospital.

Brandy found her way home and Jamie and I zoomed up to the emergency vet hospital. I stood with Coco who was in pain and held her as best as I could and engaged in prayer and healing with her. I wanted to give her a chance to recover. She was the sweetest girl in the world.

We had to leave her at the hospital and get home to our young preteen son and other animals for a few hours before we picked Coco up and transported her to my cousin's veterinary hospital. As I stepped out of the shower, I heard a loud voice in my head say as clear as day, "Do not destroy her." I was taken aback.

As we drove to the veterinary hospital, I saw signs with information. I am not one to look for signs, but it was as if the signs were coming to me and that they were there for me. One message was on a bumper sticker, and the other message was some type of an announcement on the radio. All that I can say is that I was acutely aware and paid attention to the messages that I heard and saw in a way that I never had before.

Coco received loving veterinary care that included spinal surgery and recovery for a month before she could come home. She lived for another 9 years as a disabled partially paralyzed girl hopping in our yard and around the house and was a joy to behold. I will never forget her.

What if our everyday experience of life is a limited expression of the reality of the universe? There is this synchronistic entanglement woven within the warp and weft of life. Somehow things that seem to be disparate, have a relationship and create a sense of something larger and interconnected.

It was a snowy night in the winter of 1974, my boyfriend, Barry, and I were driving back to Syracuse from Chicago where he had his medical school interview.

Before we left Syracuse, we went to say good-bye to the man who took care of Barry's hippie Volvo. The mechanic gave Barry a certain mechanical part just in case. That felt strange but okay, why not?

We were a few hours outside of Illinois, maybe in Ohio, and suddenly a dashboard light flashed on, and we knew there was a problem. We got off the highway at the next exit in the middle of nowhere. It was dark, cold, and quite snowy.

We found a gas station, where the attendant said he could fix the problem, so he did something and off we went back onto the highway. About 2 minutes later, the light went back on, so we turned around and went back to the gas station. The attendant said we would have to wait until morning so he could get a replacement part.

Out of the night, a man in what looked like a black snowsuit driving a motorcycle stopped to get gas. He came into the office where I was sitting; I mentioned what was happening. He said he was a mechanic and could fix it. Barry took out the car part and handed it to him.

The mysterious man drilled this and that and within a short time the car was fixed for good. He filled his motorcycle with gas and drove off into the night. We wanted to buy him a meal or a hot cocoa at the next service stop but we never saw him again.

It felt like we were in a dream; we were awed and happy to be back on the road again. Maybe these moments are waking us out of the dream induced state of everyday physical life and reality.

All these events opened my heart a little bit more to the reality of life. I allow myself to be more aware of synchronicity most of the time.

17

SAFETY

*"If we carry intergenerational trauma (and we do)
then we also carry intergenerational wisdom."*

~Kazu Haga

How can I feel safe when I know there is danger? That's the $5-million question and certainly one that I struggled with for a long time.

Psychologically speaking, when we are gestating inside our mother's womb and after birth, we are affected not only by the genetics of the parents but of the unhealed and unconscious traumas of the past. This transgenerational trauma gets passed down.

All people have transgenerational stresses that create the conditions for issues about safety and trust. We are all searching for safety and the ability to trust.

Unconscious survival mechanisms are the first line of defense. Our primal, animalistic instinct results in various contractions to protect our bodies, minds, and spirits.

My ancestors were not safe in the environments where they lived; hence there was the dispersion, the diaspora, throughout the European, African, and Asian continents, and later into the Western Hemisphere. This started in 586 BCE.

My great-grandparents emigrated to the United States in the late 1800s. My grandparents were born in the late 1890s or early 1900s. They maintained their Jewish identity and began to assimilate once they were in the United States. No one handed them anything; if they were successful at all, they earned it.

Even though my maternal grandfather changed his last name from Glickstein to Glendon so that people wouldn't identify him as a Jew, both branches of my families identified as Jewish and kept many of the traditions. There was a tremendous amount of antisemitism in Connecticut and New York, even though the U.S. Bill of Rights, approved in 1791, and the First Amendment of the Constitution stated that government was prohibited from impeding freedom of religion. But like today, in 2023, each state could limit the amount of freedoms people had.

Since my birth and maybe even before that, I was surrounded by and held in a field of love as well as lack of safety. For most of my life I felt unsafe. For the longest time I believed it was just how it was and that was that. As a child my defenses were to stay hidden to feel safe.

Growing up in the post-World War II years, we had air-raid drills. I remember not understanding why we had to hit the floor and try to climb under the bed. Or if I was in school why we had to go out into the hallway with our hands over our heads trying not to have my underwear show.

In those days, girls had to wear skirts to school. There was no choice.

The fear in our community was palpable. Were those drills supposed to prepare us for danger of some sort? On weekends, we ran upstairs and hid under our beds, all in an effort to prepare for nuclear bombs.

Of course, there were other reasons for the fear that surrounded me as a child. My parents had difficulties, the teachers were often mean, and one of our teachers died the same year that President Kennedy was assassinated. The images of Kennedy's death stayed with me for a long time; I still remember watching the funeral on television.

As a young girl I felt fear and kept it tucked away deep inside as I learned how to put on a false persona. As a precocious child, I developed ways to be separate from parts of myself. This made me experience a false sense of safety.

Unconsciously, I knew how to block my vulnerabilities as best as I could. I didn't want to know about them. I did everything I could to feel strong and plow ahead into the world.

Two disturbing things happened at summer camp. In the middle of the night, there was a fire on the boy's side. Somehow, we all woke up and we could see the fire across the lake. It turned out it was started in my brother's bunkhouse. In the morning they gathered the siblings together to help us feel safe. I think we were all in a state of shock.

And then, one morning I woke up and went out on the porch of the bunkhouse and saw the night watchman dead in the bushes! He was supposed to be protecting us. We never heard what had happened to him.

Sharing my fears and not keeping everything hidden, made a difference. I felt seen, heard, and loved when my parents decided to send us to a new camp the following summer.

Many years ago, I went to a workshop with Laura Davis and Ellen Bass who wrote the book, *The Courage to Heal*. They shared with us that one of their mother's listened and supported her recovery from sexual abuse and that made a huge difference in her healing and recovery.

When we are ignored or worse, blamed, the fear builds on itself and becomes toxic. When we live in a body filled with fear and stress, we are limited and the memories cycle around like a gerbil in a cage. This negatively affects the immune system and our ability to fully engage with life is impaired.

When we are seen, heard, and acknowledged, our inner environment changes, our nervous system relaxes and there is more of a chance that we can experience safety and trust. It physically changes our biochemistry and triggers feel-good, balanced chemicals. Then, it permeates through our body-mind-spirit, healing our emotions, and our immune systems.

As a teenager, I didn't want to know that I had any anxiety or fears, I wanted to be above all of that. I blamed others for my discomfort and focused on being self-reliant and self-sufficient. And it worked. I didn't want to depend on anyone. I lived and acted "as if" I were secure.

Simultaneously, I was very sociable. I had friends from school and summer camp who kept me very busy on weekends. The connections with my friends created a feeling of safety, I was part of a community and the world in a good and safe way.

In addition, I always knew and felt that I was loved. Knowing this always created a foundation for true healing to manifest as I woke up and became more conscious.

So off to college I went, focusing on psychology and anthropology. I was determined to understand what made people tick and how to create peace.

As a young woman, I was physically strong and athletic. I could sense danger from a mile away, I was hypervigilant, and my modus operandi was to stay safe with every step. I was able to trust people only after I got to know them personally. Creating connections made a difference and helped me to have a bodily sense of safety. I never dated anyone with whom I did not feel safe.

In the backdrop of my young adult years, Son of Sam was killing young woman in the 1970s and all his victims looked like me and were around my age. I needed to be careful and was always with someone when I was outside. During that time, I was deeply grateful that I was up in Syracuse.

And then, horror of horrors, the girl across the hall from me in my freshman year dormitory suddenly disappeared. Back in those days, if you wanted a ride somewhere you could post on a ride board and be matched up with others going to that same location. She wanted to go visit her boyfriend and she never arrived. The police were very busy in the dormitory interviewing us and because the case was crossing state lines the FBI was brought it. I was pretty freaked out about the whole thing.

She had come into my room that morning to ask me something and I was blank about our conversation. We never were told anything more about the incident. Decades later, when there was to be a new building erected in Syracuse, her body was finally discovered, they were able to identify her through her dental records. May Karen rest in peace and her memory be for a blessing.

In graduate school I studied counseling. After interning in a psychiatric hospital and at a residential home for boys, I didn't feel well prepared to be a counselor in the world. The internships weren't easy. I was learning on the job how to deal with very mentally and emotionally disturbed people. And I became aware of how much I didn't know.

With each course and experience I began to be more open and real and more of a compassionate person so I could be a safer counselor. To say the least, I had a lot more growing up to do. On-the-job training was much more educational than all the lectures about various situations.

After graduate school I moved back to Long Island and then to Manhattan after I landed a counseling job. I became aware of what I knew and what I didn't know. It made me feel more trustworthy when I honestly knew that I needed to immerse myself in the work itself and pursue post-graduate training.

There I was in the big city and still involved with yoga and meditation. I found out about energy healing. How lucky was I to discover Therapeutic Touch in the 1970s down at NYU? Learning about and healing blockages in the various energy centers was awesome. It helped me to connect to the sensations I had and to learn what was mine and what was someone else's. The training helped me to feel more vulnerable, more open, more real, more whole, and safer. I was able to trust myself more and felt a real strength as I counseled others.

Engaging with gestalt psychotherapy, Nondual Kabbalistic Healing_{tm}, PSYCH-K_{tm}, all sorts of meditation, energy healing, emotional freedom technique, yoga, body work, therapeutic use of essential oils, shamanistic journeying — all supported me in changing my inner environment from a fear-based field to much more optimal health which included safety and trust.

And then, on January 6, 2021, there was an insurrection at the Capitol in Washington DC. The congress was meeting to count the electoral vote to confirm the new president prior to his inauguration on January 20, 2021.

There were people wearing antisemitic T-shirts as the news described in real time what was happening with the attempted coup. I started to have an anxiety attack as if I were in imminent danger and completely powerless.

For months I knew there would be violence, I didn't know what it would be like or when. I could sense it in the air. In fact, at the end of 2020, my son mentioned something about my prediction, that the violence I had predicted had not taken place since the election and the POTUS rejecting the vote saying it was a scam.

I said, well, the inauguration isn't until January 20, 2021: anything can still happen.

I was about to give a psychotherapy healing session when a text from the *Washington Post* flashed across my phone, saying a mob had stormed into the capitol. I forwarded the text to my family. I breathed and said to myself, *"Here it is, I knew it!"*

I had to calm my anxiety and concerns during the session and I was able to focus on my client's needs. As soon as we finished, I put on the news and my anxiety was off the charts — I was in high anxiety. The representatives and senators who I respect and those who I don't respect were not safe.

I put my essential oils on to try to calm myself, I chewed on a supplement that helps with stress, I was glued to the television.

I was horrified, there was a man wearing a T-shirt saying Camp Auschwitz, I saw several others wearing shirts that read "6 M N E," meaning 6 million not enough. These people wanted us Jews dead! And they wanted others dead so they could take over. There were hardly any capitol police, one was brutally murdered, others were beaten. The air was filled with a lack of safety, racism, and lack of civility.

I was overwhelmed with fear, anxiety, and terror. Connecting with family and friends helped, but I felt powerless.

I realized I was triggered into a very deep place related to my lineage of not feeling safe. As I mentioned previously, my family left Europe in the 1800s because it was not safe to stay there anymore; this was pre-Hitler. There were pogroms — organized massacres against the Jewish communities. My families packed up and left.

I connected to the terror of my ancestors, I connected to the feeling I had of not feeling safe. I stayed with myself, I honored myself, I respected my fears, I held them close to my heart. I was with my husband and connected with my son and daughter-in-law and my friends and relatives. And then I could breathe.

I am still very affected by what goes on in the world.

Acknowledging what is happening to me, allowing contact with the fear, lack of safety, or lack of trust, makes a huge difference. As I acknowledge myself by being with myself wherever I am, I stay connected, and I feel safer.

On the spiritual level, prayer and meditation make a huge difference for my body, mind, and spirit.

I have transformed the beliefs and field I was born into. Now I live in a field of love, connection, safety, trust, and the deep allowance of imperfection.

18

TRUE INTIMACY

"Enlightenment is intimacy with all things."

~Dogen Zenji

After having a few intense relationships at a young age, I pulled way back from the world of breaking hearts and being heart-broken. My understanding of a real, good, intimate relationship was so skewed, immature, unattainable, and not enlightened at all. It was filled with childhood fantasies of Mickey and Minnie driving off in a convertible with hearts surrounding them into the sunset.

After graduate school, knowing there was so much more to discover about myself and the world, I immersed myself into my counseling job at an internationally known rehabilitation center in the heart of Manhattan. Thanks to the Theater Development Fund, I saw tons of live theatre; I saw all the foreign films as soon as they appeared at the various art houses and continued my spiritual exploration.

Getting into a relationship was on the back burner for about a minute. But for that short period of time, I put on my *"stay away from me costume"* and devoted my life to saving the world. I was constantly going on blind dates that my mother and her friends set up for me – it seemed like they had nothing better to do then try to plan my future. I didn't make it easy for the guys, I was not open and only wanted more of an intellectual free-thinking liberal kind of guy in my life.

In the back of my mind, I always knew I could join the Peace Corps if my Manhattan counseling career didn't work out. Also, I knew in my heart of hearts that one day I would get married and have children, it was a comfort that I carried with me. I just assumed it would be later on and what was the rush anyway?

It took years of consciousness-raising inner work, effort, commitment, and the intention to be authentic to realize that true intimacy — a long term, committed, respectful, mutual relationship, isn't all about sex, it is so much more! What an awakening to realize that great sex and intimacy are not the same thing.

As a young woman I was very naïve about intimacy. I thought sex and intimacy were one thing. And I believed that what I experienced sexually with a partner was the barometer that measured and rated the relationship.

Sex is fundamental to an intimate relationship, but without love, it is an objectifying experience where there is tension and no true intimacy. True intimacy is relaxing, energizing, respectful, honoring, pleasurable, playful — and there is a deeper connection.

I want to give you a bird's-eye view into what I experienced and how I healed this inner confusion and naivete.

My immature and unevolved belief about intimacy and committed relationships was that my partner should fill my emptiness and we were to give each other whatever was missing so we could feel complete. What a setup!

You give me a little loving around this and I will give you a little loving around that, you give me what I never received, and I will give you what you never received and on and on we would go, always filling each other up. We would be a team, 50% was you and 50% would be me. We would give and take, and everything would be good.

"*Danger, danger, Will Robinson!*" – *Lost In Space*

The problem was that that was an impossible task. Our internal wounded child needs healing not from another imperfect person but from our self. Our healing adult, our innate wisdom, and our spiritual selves need to learn how to fill our emptiness and heal our wounds one day at a time.

Any relationship that was based on a false philosophy was doomed to fail.

First, I had to wake up to the fact that this was what I believed and what was operating at a subconscious level. It kept me looking in all the wrong places. Waking up is hard to do and oh so necessary in order to grow together with a partner and lead a vibrant life.

After graduate school, I lived with my dog Garcia, named for Jerry, in a small one-bedroom apartment a few blocks away from the rehabilitation center where I worked. I was very busy dating.

There was another single, young woman who I was friendly with, and we spent a lot of our weekends together going to singles parties, movies, and enjoying other wonderful cultural appetizers in Manhattan. She introduced me to Jamie. Little did I know on that first night when we met at my apartment after my sign language class and his real estate class that we would be married 7 months later. That was 43 years ago and counting.

We met in February of 1979 and married in September. We were having the time of our lives. We were living the yuppie Manhattan lifestyle, two young professionals . . . I was focused on saving the world, and he was attempting to make money in the financial capital of the world.

We were falling in love, exploring our relationship and the world together. I knew I didn't want to be a wife who made my hard-earned career a side note. He was respectful of that. In fact, over these more than four decades, he has always respected my professional and personal growth endeavors.

We were individuating from our families of origin and becoming more whole; he was going to fill my unconscious needs and I was going to fill his; we didn't even know that was part of the contract, but it was.

Early on I thought that we had to be very similar, but thankfully we weren't. We had a lot of healing ground to cover and discover. We had enough similarities such as engaging in sports, politics, dancing, reading, travel, theatre, art, family, agreeing to grow through difficulties and learning to appreciate and respect each other's differences. We gave each other space to be ourselves and to spend time enjoying life together.

It was a wild and fun love affair. He loved my dog, Jamie passed that test with flying colors, and Garcia loved him. We could talk about almost anything including politics — I don't know how people who are not politically simpatico can make it. He was willing to go to the yoga ashram, we ate vegetarian food together, he met my friends and I met some of his.

We bought the Sunday *New York Times* on Saturday night after going to that movie theatre uptown that always had the best foreign films. We were able to accept and appreciate our individual differences and we were both more than eager to grow together, not that we had a clue about what that really meant! We didn't have much money, we both worked full time and before you knew it, we were married.

For 5 years everything was easy; we played, traveled, worked, and grew together. Once we became parents, things started to shift. Our preconceptions about how things should be as a husband and a wife showed up and we started to trigger each other's childhood wounds.

So, my best friend, the guy that I had so much fun with and adored and the one who I committed to for life was triggering my feelings of being ignored and misunderstood. No matter how much I was trained as a therapist and meditated and no matter how much I understood about childhood wounds and relationships, there was no stopping me from having personal reactions to certain things.

And he was triggered by me; when he was upset, he became mute, internalized everything, and couldn't connect. He would emotionally disappear.

It was easy to project what we were experiencing onto one another and besides that, we didn't know how to fight in a healthy way. We learned how, though this sounds crazy, but it was essential. We needed to be able to hate each other in order to truly love each other.

Clearly, we were reacting to our history and not able to be present all the time. We committed to being in psychotherapy for many years by connecting to the truth of our histories, feeling the discomfort of all of that and we grew closer.

We learned not to expect perfection, and that was a huge relief. We no longer expected parenting from each other. We needed to learn how to parent ourselves.

Looking back, it is clear to see how miraculous it was that we were willing and able to open the curtains of our historically blinding wounds. That created the spaciousness that allowed us to be fully present, most of the time, with each other.

I am not saying that we never get triggered by each other these days, but the turbulence gets worked through quickly and at the foundation of our relationship is a commitment to stay the course, allow dissonance, and most of all, to be honest.

We have been supportive of one another through the joyful times and through the hard, dark times. When we had difficulties, we would stay up for hours and hours at night discussing things that brought us closer together.

He watches football, I knit. He golfs, I meditate. He works in real estate and I heal. We are lovers and best friends most of the time. This is true intimacy.

19

AGGRESSION

Hansel and Gretel

The two children's wicked stepmother took them into the forest and left them there. They came upon a house made of sweets and they ate some. The evil witch that lived there locked them in a cage and was going to make a soup out of them. Gretel got out of the cage and pushed the witch into the boiling water. The children found treasure there and took it home and they were never hungry again.

In this excerpt of the *Hansel and Gretel* tale, it is clear that Gretel's escape from the cage and the pushing of the witch into the boiling water was necessary in order for the two children to live. She needed to use her innate aggression in order to escape. There was life-threatening danger there; she had to take those actions otherwise Hansel and Gretel would have been made into soup. It seems to me that the treasure Gretel found there was her ability to allow her natural expression which was absolutely necessary and fundamental for their survival.

If the development of aggression is necessary for survival on all levels, why do we have so much difficulty with aggression?

These necessary and natural tendencies are often thwarted at different stages of growth by caretakers who have difficulty bearing the aliveness of the developing, vulnerable, needy child. The aggression and difficult behaviors of the child are often met with disapproval.

Most of us are uncomfortable with our desire to destroy and kill because we don't know what to do with it.

When our natural tendencies are blocked in any way, that energy has to go somewhere. When blocked, development is distorted, uneven, unnatural, and can develop into harmful behaviors. The child's natural will becomes confused.

There are also aggressive forces that we experience daily that are the expressions of the desire to move into and interact with others and the environment. When we are hungry, we need to eat, when we are tired, we need to rest, when we are thirsty, we need to drink, when we are lonely, we need to connect, when we need to go to the bathroom, we need to go.

When there is too much focus on bringing a child up to be good, respectful, appreciative, and not questioning of authority in any way, there are often problems because the child doesn't learn to question or to have their own creative ideas or intuition. Their actions have to pass through an approval screen before they act on them.

Subsequently, the child learns to control and divert their primal instincts and needs which leads to all sorts of physical problems and neuroses.

Taking aggressive actions is necessary for a healthy development. Just think of chewing food; we need to deconstruct whatever we are eating in order for the nutrients to assimilate, to metabolize them into energy and to release the toxins.

Anger was rarely expressed in my childhood home and when it was, it brought up fear in me. I didn't know how to assimilate it. The message to me was, "*If you don't have anything nice to say, don't say it.*" I needed to be a "*good girl,*" which meant that I shouldn't express myself or I may have been perceived as "*not nice.*" And I didn't want love to be taken away from me.

For the longest time I believed that having and experiencing aggression was bad and that it was a replacement for something else I didn't want to experience. I truly didn't believe it was an innate power. Consequently, I created ways to get rid of and eliminate it from my consciousness. After all, if I expressed aggression in an unacceptable way, that would leave a negative mark on my soul.

Anger was taboo, being accepted and loved was my goal. Just the thought of being out of control and my fear of impending disapproval reinforced my inhibitions. My self-esteem was confused because I couldn't allow myself to know about my needs. I became a master of focusing on others.

Little did I know that all those behaviors were controlling my natural rhythm. What remained was a conundrum: how do I live optimally with these powerful forces streaming through my body? Anger, what's that? What in the world do I do when my aggression arises? After all, it's powerful stuff and I could really hurt someone, let alone hurt myself. So, I silenced myself most of the time.

When my hormones started to rush though my body, I was no longer able to control what was happening inside me. Suddenly I was alive, wild, expressive, and angry. I was at a loss, and I no longer cared.

During those teenage years, I acted out a lot of my aggression because I didn't know how to express it after having distorted it for so long. My internal training unraveled, although I attempted to be polite in many situations even when I was fuming inside.

I had no idea how to express anger it was trial-and-error for a long time. Obviously, I had a lot of aggression stored up in me over the years from holding in, holding back, and molding myself into a plastic Barbie doll.

As I realized that having aggression is natural, I started to develop a relationship with what was happening in my body and my mind. I started to channel it in healthier ways; through physical exercise, I learned the importance of really chewing my food. But something was still off.

I needed to get to the root of how I exiled this necessary, life affirming aggression. I wanted to express what arose in me more naturally, and I was stuck. I needed help. I couldn't do it alone.

Buddhism teaches us about suffering. It acknowledges that life always involves suffering at different levels, it teaches about the origin of suffering, the end of suffering and then freedom from suffering. There is so much wisdom in those seemingly simple *Four Noble Truths*.

So, I decided to develop more of a relationship with my suffering through psychotherapy. Since I had blind spots, my therapist helped me wake up to how I was defending myself and not fully living.

I entered into a darkness that seemingly had no light in it. In that place, I felt completely separate. Connecting to my history, to my lineage, and most importantly, to my body brought me into communion with aspects of myself that I had exiled. As I stayed there and was present in that hidden, shadowy place, more breath and light began to emerge. I became the phoenix rising through the ashes.

There were internal crevices in which I had hidden vulnerability, fragility, desires, and needs. Steadily, though, I developed a relationship with them by giving them a home in my heart. It was awesome to truly pay attention to myself and not disregard my thoughts, emotions, or physical sensations. Some of the thoughts were judgmental, some were creative and some of them were just distractions. It made a colossal difference to hear myself, pay attention and to be respectful of what emerged.

Even though anger and aggression are natural, they can be dangerous if not respected. I learned how to respect them and I felt stronger, more integrated and alive as I acknowledged this part of me.

The primal forces of aggression are extremely powerful and need to be respected.

When I consciously related to my aggression, I needed to heal my fear of its destructive power. Eventually, I learned how to appreciate my aggression, how to relate to it and how to express myself wholeheartedly from it. Sometimes, it's necessary to express the feelings to someone that hurt you and sometimes it's better not to. There isn't a template that describes exactly when. It is all about becoming more discerning.

I received guidance from aggression's innate wisdom. In the past when I disregarded it, I was only hurting myself and others. I learned how I was projecting outward onto others and how I was living with false beliefs about life. The more I took responsibility and connected with my suffering and the sensations in my body, the more I became truly alive and compassionate.

As I connected with all aspects of myself, I was able to know when I was triggered and to where I had been triggered. First, I needed to remember that if I was having a strong reaction, that I was usually being triggered into my past. After connecting with the past, I would focus on my needs. Then I would decide if I wanted to have a conversation with the person who triggered me.

In the beginning of this whole healing process, when I was uncomfortable about confronting someone, I would put my hand on my heart and speak honestly and slowly. Acknowledging my discomfort and my heart really helped me feel centered and present.

Some people say you have to be calm to express your anger. I disagree. I think we need to be in relationship with what is happening; if someone is in danger you shouldn't wait to calm down, you must act in the moment and be clear. We have to assess what is needed and the path of right action.

The truth is, aggression is empowering when we develop a relationship with it and it becomes integrated into who we are.

20

UNCERTAINTY

"Certainty is the death of wisdom, thought, creativity."

~Shakar Kapur

Wars, a pandemic, politics, mass murders, racism, the rise of antisemitism, people scamming. These disturbing events bring me into the depths of my being and into places I haven't always traversed.

Uncertainty is an intrinsic part of the warp and weft of life. Quantum physics tells us that it is built into reality.

Uncertainty is often seen as the enemy. Fundamentalism wants to eradicate it through its dogma.

We can't get around it, we can't control it, we never know when we will experience it. When we do, it can open us to the vulnerability of life as it is.

For decades I preferred to be entranced by the illusion of certainty. I wanted to avoid my fears. I avoided it by shape-shifting; I altered my form to be less in touch. I lived in a historical trance. I saw life with partial vision. My view of reality was distorted.

I wanted to quantify things to feel safe in my attempt to be certain. I created pseudo-certainties and pseudo-safeties for survival in order to navigate in the world. Because of these historically necessary coping and survival patterns, I clearly altered reality and lived entranced. I split from places that I deemed unacceptable and thus I lived with limited vision, perception, awareness, consciousness, and compassion.

When I avoided the abiding truth of uncertainty, I was affected in the various realms—physically, emotionally, mentally, and spiritually.

My intention in this life has been to be in a deep relationship with the truth and reality, so I needed to develop new muscles to meet and touch uncertainty. I longed to be real and whole. Since wholeness includes uncertainty, I needed to look through a different lens, one that wasn't created from history and memory.

For lifetimes, I prayed to live the truth of reality. What I discovered was that my failures proved to be a doorway into a new world filled with the vibrancy of suffering and joy. So, I committed to being directly in relationship with the contradictions of life, the unknown and the great uncertainty.

It hasn't been easy.

Uncertainty took me directly into the unknown of life and death that is always present. I chose to open the curtain and experience reality more and more. I have experienced whatever arises, be it confusion, clarity, vulnerabilities, real strengths, along with joys and sorrows.

Here's what I discovered:

I was leaving out parts of myself by avoiding and holding my fears captive.

As an experienced psychotherapist, I felt certainty most of the time in the many ways of connecting clients with their histories, remembering their stories, opening to their bodies, and returning to more of a natural state of elan vital, the full life force. I traveled in the unknown quite a bit, but it was different because I didn't include uncertainty and my personal response to it. Clients healed, yet there was less awakening.

As I traversed the territory from a more integrated perspective as a nondual healer, I included more of myself and was filled with a depth of uncertainty that I had never embraced before. I had more anxiety and simultaneously, I was much more present. Clients had so many more transformational experiences through their healing sessions when I embodied all of who I am.

Now, I intentionally step into the river of uncertainty and ride on the pulsating life force of healing. It is infinitely dimensional as we venture inside of it. Sometimes it feels dangerous to enter the river where I engage with the primal and unadorned forces of life, because there are no fixed rules and there is nothing to grasp onto.

I never know what will rise up in the river. What is the temperature of the water? What is the current like today? Will I encounter the river's angels and/or its demons? What debris will be rising to the surface today?

Sometimes, it dredges up the monsters that live on the bottom of the river.

Allowing myself to ride in the unknown, including uncertainty, not controlling what surfaced and what I needed to contact, has been a creative process. My heart, mind, intuition, and curiosity guide me.

I take the whole person in; I include myself and whatever comes up. Paradoxically, I am in more of a relationship when I don't use any fixed ideologies or prescribed techniques to organize what is unknown and uncertain.

Now healing sessions are much more transformational, fully relational, deeply awakening, and healing.

I include more and more of what arises through stepping into and out of the river.

I allow a relationship with the uncertainty of life and death to grow and blossom.

This process has healed me as well as my clients.

I include my mind and my heart along with uncertainty. I breathe with life more.

Sometimes it brings up ancient wounds and a variety of other emotions and sensations.

Allowing myself to walk in and step out of the river has given way to the birth of new certainty, intimacy, and presence. In this place, life and death dance together and make love.

I don't believe it's about becoming comfortable with uncertainty; it's about having a relationship with it. I include my human frailties, imperfections, strengths, and wisdom.

Sometimes I am more uncomfortable and more present, at other times I am settled and at times I feel unsettled.

As I step in and out of the river, kindness is fundamental to this level of healing and practice.

I do not sit on top of a mountain chanting *Om*, although occasionally it is good to do that. I am in and of the world. I include what arises through stepping into and out of the river and allowing a relationship with uncertainty to grow. This helps me to be embodied as a healing presence and be who I am.

About seven years ago, a new client walked into my office. She sat down on the couch across from me and told me that her doctors had given her a year to live. She wanted to know what I could do to heal her, she wasn't ready to die, as she was in her early 50s.

So, the first thing I allowed in was my anxiety, shock, and fear. I was swimming in uncertain thoughts: How can I be here for this woman? What is healing? I was aware of my grandiosity; can I make this cancer disappear? Can I save her life? And then I stood in the river of the uncertainty of her life and the uncertainty of my life ... and the healing began.

As difficult as this was, I knew that my wrestling and presence was transformational. As I included all my feelings, thoughts, sensations, and desires, I was able to settle in, remember and realize that I could be here for her emotionally and spiritually.

This realization was from a form of certainty that rose inside of me, I knew there could be healing and awakening. By including all my thoughts, feelings, and sensations, I remembered and had access to more of myself and opened the gate of compassion and the doors of perception.

My client lived another 3 years and was able to experience emotional and spiritual healing as well as prepare for her death.

Walking in the river and engaging with the uncertainty that lives there has brought up my doubt, anxiety, self-judgment, rage, sexual feelings, confusion, insecurity, and inadequacies. The more I remember the reality of uncertainty as an intrinsic part of nature, the more I am a healing presence.

This journey cannot be done without friends and kindness toward ourselves.

21

SEPARATION

"We are here to awaken from our illusion of separation."

~Thich Nhat Hanh

Our greatest suffering is our sense of separateness. Separate from all of who we are, separate from God, reality, wholeness, and the truth.

Some religions talk about the fall from grace, evil, brokenness, or not being in harmony with nature. Psychologically, we experience the sense of separateness as utter loneliness, despair, and alienation.

My belief was that wholeness was something I needed to search for and work hard to attain. So, I went on vision quest after vision quest in search of the holy Shangri-La, the mystical city, assuming that my answer was outside of me somewhere far away.

I struggled to find the answer as if there were one answer that would satisfy me and help me to become fully myself. I wanted a map! Much to my dismay, there wasn't any.

Becoming real is different for each one of us. I kept arriving at dead ends. I often thought, as Jack Nicholson said in the movie with Helen Hunt, *"Is this as good as it gets?"* In fact, that was the name of the movie.

In my gut and heart of hearts, I knew there was more and that I couldn't do it alone. And I absolutely needed to go beyond psychotherapy!!

A lot of the healing and spiritual workshops I attended taught ways to maintain separateness and not be in relationship with my authentic self. Sounds crazy? It was crazy! The belief was that if you merge with the oneness and eradicate the ego, that was the key to unlock the gates of heaven on Earth.

I longed to be unified and whole, so I meditated and merged with oneness attempting to get rid of my "ego." Of course, that didn't work.

Jason Shulman, the founder of Nondual Kabbalistic Healing_tm, taught that we need to heal our egos, not exile them. Whoa!! What?! That stopped me in my tracks.

Suddenly, I was at a fork in the road and turned onto a new path, oh my! I resonated with it, I felt "gotten." Something was different this time. I didn't have to do anything extreme except engage with spiritual practice and heal through the de-constructing of preconceptions, pulling back the curtain, opening the doors of perception and being in relationship with myself, others and the reality of life that has always been here. I figured I could do that.

In 2002, I was at a spiritual practice retreat, led by Jason, on a beautiful campus in New England. Trees, grass, streams, birds, little critters, fresh clean air, and lots of space. All of the participants were students and graduates of the various courses offered at A Society of Souls, the School for Nondual Healing and Awakening_tm. We were kindred spirits, all of us deeply committed to healing and awakening. And luckily, since it was a small retreat center, we were the only group there.

I couldn't ask for any environment much better than that. I knew many of the people there, intimately. My roommate and I were very close at that time. I was safe.

The theme of the retreat focused on a spiritual practice that supported our exploration of the existential questions of life and death through engagement with varying states of embodied consciousness. Our healing egos were included as we explored many vistas of spaciousness and return to the heart.

We practiced throughout the day and evening, we shared, we laughed, we cried, and we ate together. There were periods of silence and blocks of time where we could explore the grounds, practice, nap, write, paint, or do whatever we wanted and needed.

The practice brought me to moments of realization, wholeness, and a sense of integration. It was just what I needed. I was happy. After all, that was what all the healing, practice, longing, and searching had been for. I felt freer than ever.

And then, the day before the end of the retreat, I felt awful. I wasn't physically ill, but I just didn't feel comfortable in my own skin. There was an incredible sense of separation from myself, from my friends, from everything. Honestly, I was anxious about the state of disconnect in which I found myself. And, I stayed with it.

My longing to be whole brought me to this place. All the psychological and spiritual work I had engaged with for many decades gathered the pieces of my personal self to the moment where I could actually feel the depth of my suffering, a total sense of separateness.

I knew that I needed to be where I was. And, it wasn't easy.

I kept practicing and spent a lot of time by myself. I couldn't relate to anyone else, so it just seemed wiser to go with the powerful sense of separateness. I wrote and drew in my journal. I practiced and sat in nature among the trees. I prayed and gazed into the space that was filled with the streaming pulsations of life.

Even though I was feeling profoundly separate, as if I were suddenly completely alone on an island far, far away, I was able to respond to people if they spoke with me. The request for silence during the retreat helped to support me to be where I was and transform the profound separateness I had clearly suffered from for eons.

The next morning, we all gathered to share and ask questions as we prepared to leave the retreat. Timidly, I raised my hand and shared about how separate I felt and how hard it had been for me. Allowing myself to be vulnerable and express my difficulty, allowing myself to be in relationship with my suffering on Saturday, and being heard by this community, shifted me. I started to feel human again, and slowly took one step after another into the world. It was remarkable.

Naming, acknowledging, sharing, being heard, a safe space, a provocative healing modality, a beautiful environment — all these conditions created the space for my internal shift into more of my true authentic nature.

I felt a meeting of my spiritual self and my personal self in a huge way, as if I were being held with all of me and more. The spiritual and the material met inside my body, mind, and spirit.

My heart opened as I realized I had found a place where I could be an imperfect human being who can heal and be truly present, whole, real, and compassionate.

Some nondual spiritual teachers say there is nothing to do since we are already whole. I disagree with that. There is a lot of healing we need to do to heal our suffering and to open our hearts in order to embody the wholeness that we are.

Suzuki Roshi, a Soto Zen monk who popularized Buddhism and started the San Francisco Zen Center and Tassajara, said, *"Each of you is perfect the way you are, and you can use a little improvement."*

My heart was filled with a creative emptiness, a quiet inner peaceful freedom and joy. I was home in my heart.

My awakening has been to continuously realize on every level — mind, body, heart, and spirit — that there is an interconnectedness of all things and I am not separate.

The nondual nature of life is so large, it absolutely includes duality. I am healing and awakening. I am here now. May we all be blessed.

22

MEDITATION

*"In the beginner's mind there are many possibilities,
in the expert's there are few."*

~Shunyro Suzuki

For years, as I sat on a pillow with legs crossed, I believed I was supposed to reach a state of no thoughts. *Zen Mind Beginner's Mind* by Suzuki Roshi, of the San Francisco Zen Center, was my bible. That was a big relief especially since I was truly a beginner back in 1973.

Luckily, I opened into the state of beginner's mind. Remembering that I didn't have to know what I didn't know, and that I could fail, feel lost, and be confused was profoundly healing. Just that made a huge difference in my life, since I was being with whatever showed up even though I didn't like it.

My hidden goal was to be successful at meditation even when I couldn't reach the state of no thoughts. I failed over and over and even though I was relieved to be a beginner, I became anxious, agitated, annoyed, and frustrated that I couldn't reach my goal after so many years.

Even though I failed at attaining my goal, I kept reminding myself that I was cultivating something indescribable through sitting. I knew there was wisdom embedded within the practice even though I didn't feel very wise.

For years, I continued failing and I kept practicing. Even so, I was magnetically drawn to practice, I felt at home. My experiences with so much failure healed me, and I no longer feared making mistakes in the same way. I am not saying that I don't get activated at times by making mistakes but quite honestly, I have more inner peace in relationship to it.

Why did I continue? Dogen Zenji, who lived from 1200-1253, was a Japanese Buddhist priest and the founder of Soto Zen in Japan. He taught zazen, also known as sitting meditation. Within his scholarly teachings of the "*Shobogenzo*", he taught that "*practice is enlightenment.*"

Looking back now, what I know is that I entered the field of enlightenment each time I sat down to practice. After practice, I always felt better, even though "nothing" was happening except for the constant presence of thoughts and what seemed to be lengthy discussions about this or that. My mind was so busy and crazy, the never-ending thoughts were tied together like a beautiful strand of pearls.

This state of consciousness was revealing something to me.

Early on, when I arrived at moments of nothingness, as I experienced a brief opening into another world, I would quickly close the curtains and go back to what I knew. I started to pay attention to that, as it was healing just to notice my process.

Something was happening within me even with all the coming and going. I felt more stable, more connected, more in touch, my mind was clearing up and I had more vitality. And the best part of it all, is that I was more present.

There were many times over the years when I seriously considered not continuing with meditation.

As I went deeper into the practice, however, the thoughts appeared to rise up from a deep well inside of me. Somehow it seemed like the well was even deeper than from this life, maybe it was a connection to my lineage, maybe past lives. In the unknown space, I began to make connections and have insights, whether true or not. It wasn't all suffering and dark. The more I was with whatever showed up, the more present I was after the practice.

It took a while, and then my attitude started changing. It no longer mattered that my thoughts kept rising up, that's just what happens. It's part of being human. Miraculously, by allowing all the thoughts and the wild stuff from deep inside to surface I became calmer. I was changing.

My awakening was very gradual; no big revelations, just being in the practice. Clearly there were changes in my brain, my heart, my body, and in my emotions.

There was a spaciousness that simultaneously grew inside and around me. I was being carried on the wings of Presence. The spaciousness became the foreground, and my thoughts became the background. Incredible. At that point I became even more committed to regular practice.

My cup had been so full, it was overflowing for what seemed like an eternity. As my cup started emptying, it became clear that I was training to be in the unknown and more in reality. In that place, I was able to experience more of the continuity of life as it is. Yeah!

It took me about ten years of regular practice to experience what I defined as a breakthrough, and it wasn't merging into the oneness. I still had loads of thoughts and yet I developed a different relationship to them all and to myself. The fight to get rid of thoughts diminished. I experienced more spaciousness; I was calmer and more centered. I sensed that all of that being with the turbulence and allowing failure was the portal to opening my heart and developing true compassion.

Over the years, I experimented with Vipassana meditation, yogic meditations, Zazen, guided meditations, breath meditation, Kabbalistic meditation, walking meditation, moving meditations, relaxation, visualization and probably a few others.

Wherever I am I will meditate at some point during the day. I used to prefer if there were no distractions and honestly, I prefer to be in a quiet space or in nature with the sounds of the birds. A lot of the time I am dealing with the noises of life, a truck passing by, construction, lawn mowers, sirens, trains, and cats fighting. Yet, I continue to practice.

About 20 years ago, I went through a very stressful few years with my parents becoming ill and dying. Every day, I practiced. I sat myself down and closed my eyes and meditated.

Even when I took them to doctor's appointments and made trips to the emergency room, I practiced. During those tough times, I mediated more than once a day, even if it was for just a few minutes at a time. It didn't matter whether I reached this state or that state; what mattered was that I experienced an inner and outer support that helped to save my sanity and my body. And it helped me to make informed life-and-death decisions.

Meditation brought me home to myself. Studies show that meditation changes our brain, helps with physical issues and with stress. Research has also shown that meditation improves the immune system, can stabilize blood pressure, transform stress, increase cognitive ability, strengthen focus, produce a feeling of centeredness, and integrate mind, body, and spirit.

Meditation changed my life, it brought me into the stream of true heart-centered compassion by riding the huge waves of my thoughts, preconceptions, and love. I keep returning to myself and the here-and-now.

For me this is freedom, giving myself choices about where to be, rather than how to be. Really the only demand on myself is to be myself.

I'm more real and happier, I love more, and I grieve more. Everything I do is more present centered. It wasn't easy to get here. I have gone through the dark night of the soul and now I am mostly living in the light of love and gratitude.

I sit and I am just where I am. I breathe naturally and I am with whatever shows up. Sometimes I still have an active mind. Each practice is different.

Meditation changes me and creates the conditions for a more centered day most of the time. And then, life's comings and goings cause changes. That's just how it is.

I am freer with that attitude.

After years of attempting to attain a certain state of enlightenment through meditation, I began to rest in the spaciousness of what I have always been a part of and didn't realize.

Each moment is different, each breath is different, and when I can just be with that, I can just be where I am.

I am able to face the present moment more gently and with full embodied presence most of the time now.

Meditation doesn't take away our difficulties, but it changes us with each moment of direct "here-ness" and presence.

I have more pleasure and more pain, each thing becomes itself, the turbulence of difficulty is the difficulty, and the joy is the joy.

Meditation isn't about getting rid of suffering; it's about being where we are so that we can find the wisdom in it and be open-hearted to whatever we traverse.

Meditation cultivates our ability to be truly human with all the frailties and strengths we have and to be with life one moment at a time.

It helps to practice with friends.

I no longer have the longing to escape life and merge with the oneness. What I have realized is that wherever I am, I am a part of the oneness and being in life is what I care about the most.

23

NOURISHMENT

"When you find what you love, you do it. That's it."

~Elizabeth Holzman

The flight attendant instructed us to put the oxygen mask on first before we put it on our child or someone else in need.

I had heard this hundreds of times before, but I never really listened and received the message. This time I heard what I was being told. It was quite simple and profound.

This meant that I must put the oxygen mask on first before putting it on my child. I was shocked.

What, me first? I thought the baby was supposed to come first. Any good parent would want to have their child get oxygen as soon as possible.

What, what, what? Nope, that wasn't the truth, I was living in a fantasy and a lie. The truth is just the opposite. Take care of yourself, then take care of the child.

This was all about real fundamental survival. If I run out of oxygen, I can't help anyone else.

There was no turning back. Seriously, this was a big deal for me.

Waking up to reality comes in different ways. I wasn't prepared for the portal into the truth to look like this. So much for preconceived notions about awakening. Got it.

For forever and a day, I believed that I should take care of others before I even thought about myself. After all, thinking about myself was selfish.

Most of the time, I was very successful at taking care of others. Until I needed to change.

By attending to myself first, it ensured that I would have the mental and physical facilities needed to take care of my child. I was really shaken up. It was good, I needed to be shaken up. After all, I had longed to be whole. I had prayed to wake up to reality. So here it was, a wakeup call, a huge, loud message.

It felt like I was hit by lightning. In a flash, I transformed some deeply ingrained belief systems that went something like this: I would give my life up for my son. Wouldn't any good parent sacrifice their life for their child?

The puzzle pieces started to become chaotic; where and how do I fit this new revelation into my being and into my heart. What in the world does this really mean? What is the ramification of it all? How am I going to live with this new awareness?

A lot of ways I had functioned as a person in the world were backwards and inside out. How could this be? I had gotten so far walking upside down and inside out. I needed to truly realize that and allow the discomfort and the sense of discombobulation to truly change me.

I realized I had been giving myself away to be seen a certain way, maybe to try to erroneously control others' opinions of me, all in an effort to stay safe. I was done with all of that, finished. I wanted to be the best mom and person I could possibly be and that meant waking up and receiving messages from others, the world, and from inside myself in ways that I had not planned. This was what I had asked for, so I was willing to experience vulnerability and open my heart.

This was all about true nourishment.

Nourishment, I was so confused about that. All the therapies and new-agey stuff said you must love yourself first, that sounded great in theory but at first, I didn't know how to do it. If I drew a cartoon of myself in that moment it would have been with two heads on top of a very long neck looking like clowns and facing in opposite directions. Yup, to me nourishment meant to take care of others first and then maybe think about myself.

I seriously took all of this to heart; learning how to nourish myself was a huge undertaking. It meant really looking at myself: how I lived, what I believed, getting support from a psychotherapist, engaging with spiritual practice, and changing at a fundamental level. And then allowing the discomfort of change, not an easy thing to do but necessary to traverse the transitional space of newness and integration. It just felt so weird and yet it gave me more freedom every step of the way.

The typical definition of "nourishment" is the food or other substances necessary for growth, health, and good condition. Supporting our bodies with proper foods and nutrition is essential for the stability necessary for engaging with life. Over the years I have completely changed how I approach nourishment, what I eat and how I eat, in a conscious way.

I pay attention to what my body wants and needs in that moment. As I feed my body, I am nourishing it. When I take the time to inquire where I am and what I need, it makes a huge difference. Sometimes, I will engage in conscious emotional eating, because just being conscious makes a difference.

There is so much more to nourishment than what we eat and put into our bodies. It is the ability to take in life in a way that is sustaining on all levels: physically, emotionally, mentally, and spiritually.

Psychotherapy helped me to wake up, and I completely changed how I lived. I remembered what I did to survive and then I was able to go beyond the story of my history and connect with more reality as a source of inner strength, become embodied and just be my imperfect human self.

So, what is healthy nourishment? To me, the answer is pleasure. When I consciously pay attention to my needs, the nourishment I take in is rich, even when it is a simple gesture.

As I consciously nourished myself, I experienced how it fed my soul, my body, my heart, and my mind. I didn't leave any part of myself out. I experienced wholeness more and more as I integrated all of myself and paid attention to my physical, emotional, and spiritual needs.

Knitting has been creative nourishment for me since I was in Girl Scouts in elementary school. My mom and my piano teacher, Gloria, were our Girl Scout leaders. So, knitting was a connection I had with my mom. We spent a lot of hours creating together, for the rest of her life.

Choosing a pattern is a lot of fun. There are so many we have access to these days because of the internet, Ravelry (a website for knitting and crocheting- https://www.ravelry.com/about), makers' websites, and social media. Knitting has connected me to the world in a unique, beautiful way.

The fibers, the colors, how the yarns are spun, the various embellishments within the fibers are such a delight. Touching the wool, cashmere, yak, alpaca, cotton, and all kinds of hand-dyed combinations and different bases is so pleasurable. Some of the yarns are so sensual they elicit a connection to the animals whose coats were shaved to become the glorious fibers used for knitting.

One of my favorite knitting companies based in the United States, *Knit Collage (https://knitcollage.com/)*, employs women in India to spin and create magnificent yarns. The owner, Amy Small (@knitcollage), gathers ribbons and trinkets from the markets in India, then they are included into the yarns when the women spin them. They bring me so much joy. I don't know if I will ever travel to India, yet I get to experience through the yarn a small piece of the wisdom and love of beauty existing in that part of the world.

Once I choose the yarns and the patterns, I simply use two long needles and wind the yarn in either this direction or that direction and voila I have a knit or a purl stitch. As I follow the pattern stitch by stitch and row by row, trying to make as few mistakes as possible, I eventually complete the garment. Even though I follow a pattern created by a maker, the yarns I choose to use, and how I put it all together makes it an original creation; wearing it or giving it as a gift gives me so much pleasure. This is true creative nourishment for me.

As the natural health world grew, I grew with it. I learned and studied about homeopathy, cell salts, herbs, vitamins, minerals, fasting, detoxing, and even wheatgrass. I always tried everything first before bringing it home for the family or recommending something to a client. I was my own guinea pig.

Essential oils have nourished me for the past 36 years. I had always been intrigued by natural plant medicine. Through some training I found there are so many biochemical and therapeutic properties that change our energy as soon as we smell them and layer them onto our body. I put a blend of oils from trees on the bottom of my feet each morning for balance and grounding, and then a few drops of a citrus oil blend to strengthen my energy, I put another oil from flowers, ylang ylang, on my heart center, and upon waking up, I use a combination of oils to energize me on all the other levels for the day.

Sometimes I even put a few drops into a capsule and swallow that as a supplement. My favorites to take internally are oregano and lemongrass for their antiviral benefits. Since a little oil can make a big impact, I use them religiously. I travel with them, I exercise with them, I teach with them, and I also use them to guide and support people on their healing path.

Lavender was my first exposure to essential oils. Someone handed me a bottle and said, "Smell this, it will relax you." And it did.

Soon the whole house smelled like lavender: lavender heart potpourri, lavender baths, lavender on the sheets and pillowcases, lavender deodorant, lavender pancakes, lavender everything — until I found out there were many more essential oils than lavender — a lot more!

I was insatiable and had to learn about every one of them. One by one, I had to try them all on myself and with my son. You name it, we tried it. Oils for tummy aches, for nap time, boo-boos and to help with focus.

That was the beginning of my essential oil journey and a way I nourish myself and others all the time.

Whether painting or knitting, collaging, cooking, baking, or doing some type of movement, I make it mine. I follow my own rhythm and that is what is so nourishing for me.

Reading, going to museums, teaching, seeing theatre, watching movies, occasionally eating at a really good restaurant, meditating, exercising, collaging, playing games, walking, watching favorite television programs, studying, learning, window shopping, giving healing sessions, listening to podcasts, following various artists on Instagram, traveling, painting, taking baths, getting a massage, organizing, connecting with family and friends, spending some time alone.

These are some of the many ways I nourish myself.

So, I get it. Putting the oxygen mask on myself first, I am more nourished, and I can meet each moment as it arises.

24

STOPPING AND TURNING
INTO MYSELF

*"The best and most beautiful things in the world cannot be
seen or even touched —they must be felt with the heart."*

~The Little Prince

During graduate school, I went in a new direction.
I was completely committed to saving the world,
so I was thrilled with my studies and internships. I
devoted myself to studying, writing, meditation, yoga, dating, and going for walks with my amazing dog, Garcia. My
focus was on deepening my ability to be a healing presence
for people.

Experimenting with drugs was a thing of the past.

After graduation, I was lucky to land a job in the
vocational rehabilitation program at the International
Center for the Disabled, a well-known rehabilitation center in Manhattan. There was a wonderful mix of 20 and
30 year olds who were developing their careers and lives.
Together, we were growing up and learning about life, terrible suffering, healing, and the world.

The work was intense; hundreds of emotionally and physically disabled people passed through our small evaluation and training program each year. We supported our clients to explore training and educational programs, offered emotional interventions, placement preparation, and ancillary medical services.

It was on-the-job training. All my graduate training didn't prepare me for what I encountered. Day after day, my heart broke for so many clients. My compassion grew exponentially as I wrestled with many of the traumas and stories I heard about.

I taught myself about opening and deep listening, hearing, and taking people in. I learned about what it was like to grow up with a psychotic mother and how she was repeatedly abused by the priest. I didn't want to believe her, but I did. I learned about surviving a suicide attempt and ending up severely physically impaired. I learned about Alzheimer's disease in a 56-year-old professor from an Ivy League school. Alzheimer's wasn't even in the news yet — and I wanted to cry with his wife. I took a suicidal woman to the hospital and sat there for hours to get her admitted. I worked with a man who had a stroke and lost his life's work. I learned about some of the most strange and unusual conditions that left people's lives devastated. I worked with two people who were transitioning their gender identity. I learned about rape. One client was a murderer, and I didn't want to work with him. Those are just a few of the hundreds of people I worked with and met heart-to-heart over those years.

Thankfully the staff shared together, but I needed more. Much more.

After several years, the internal politics at the agency grew worse, and everyone was not on the same page. All of us were over-worked and underpaid.

There were way too many administrators. Even though I loved the counseling and most of the staff, the atmosphere of the institute became filled with conflict, control, mind games, and tons of inequity.

I became a shop steward for the union and got enmeshed in trying to make changes. Then I became even more stressed, and I just wasn't happy. I was in my twenties. Something was missing at the institute and within me. Little did I know that what was missing was a lot of me.

I had done a lot of soul-searching over the years but not enough. I was very unevenly developed. I needed to wake up!

My personal life was good. I was still meditating and doing a lot of yoga. Unfortunately, there weren't any yoga studios back in those days. Weiser's bookstore, a famous spiritually oriented book publisher and bookstore, was near to my apartment so I spent a lot of time there, feeling my connection with like-minded people. I dated a lot and met my wonderful husband on a blind date.

I needed answers, I needed a path, I needed help.

Occasionally, I used drugs in an attempt to replicate the wisdom I received during some of the peak experiences I had had when experimenting with psychedelics.

I wanted to escape the madness of everyday life.

I realized that if I were to walk my walk and talk my talk and truly be a healing presence in the world, I had to stop using drugs and dive deeper into self-inquiry and consciousness raising.

I prayed for guidance.

One day when I was at work, I decided to get a drink of water and take a stretch. For no apparent reason I paid a certain type of pointed attention to a man who was in the program. He was nodding and falling out of his seat because he was so stoned. I had seen others doing this many times over the years, but the difference that day was within me.

It was right smack in the middle of the day and life at work. In a flash, it was as if an invisible door opened, and I stepped into it. I had prepared to enter that portal for so long. It was time. I was in a time-space warp, everything slowed down around me as I stood there, receiving a download of information about myself and life and what I needed to do.

In that moment I knew I had a significant life purpose as a healing presence, I absolutely needed to change and grow.

I had been questioning everything for years. I think it may be that I was working so intensely with being of service to clients who attended the rehabilitation center that my heart was opening, and I was becoming more aware of the places where I was blocked and lonely and still frozen in history.

All of this happened in a flash of realization. I felt I was being guided by an angel. I didn't even believe in angels or beings from other dimensions at that time. Whenever I described the story of what I experienced, I said that an angel was with me or visited me.

I felt as if I were being shown the direction to walk in and quite honestly, I have never looked back since that moment.

I stopped, and turned toward myself and the reality I was searching for. I went in a new direction, deeper inside of myself through natural means.

I felt supported. I was shown there is a path for me, and it would unfold as I went deeper into myself. My senses were heightened, the doors of perception opened wide, and the crisp air filled and surrounded me. I was not alone.

This all happened in a moment in time. At first, I thought it was a flashback.

Immediately, I walked into another room and put my hand on a drafting table to stabilize myself but realized something was really happening. I couldn't wait to go home and tell Jamie.

At that point in my life, I was in relationship with some of my emotional, mental, and spiritual baggage, but there was a whole arsenal to uncover and realize. And of course, I now know that healing our hearts and souls is a lifelong process that takes deep commitment to being with the truth and transforming it.

It took me a while to embrace the true path of soul healing, even though I wanted to get there as quickly as possible.

I just knew there was more to life than what I was aware of at that point. I have healed in ways and on levels I didn't even know were possible but that took a lot of perseverance and stopping the madness to be able to realize and receive who I am and who I was born to be.

At first, my intention was to rise to a higher state of consciousness. Yes, that sounds like someone who loved hallucinogens! But what I really needed was to go down and turn into myself in a new way. It was as if I were waiting for myself all those years – or who knows, maybe lifetimes. I was being guided by my higher wisdom.

I had been reevaluating the purpose of life for years and working hard at finding my place in it all.

I started to connect more to my inner wisdom, knowing and realizing as well how much I didn't know.

Healing my tender heart was the most natural and wonderful thing I have done and then again it was one of the most difficult things.

I had fertilized the ground so much at that point that there was enough of me sprouting and ready to jump into myself and start being myself. It was time and way overdue.

I discovered a new awareness of reality in relation to myself.

The whole is greater than the sum of its parts.

For decades now, I have touched and perceived the pulsating stream of reality without drugs. Instead, I engage with writing, meditation, prayer, and other spiritual processes. This has made a difference in my life in ways that have been remarkable.

This stopping shook me awake! I stood fully in myself and said "hineni," Hebrew for "I AM Here". Here I am, and I am buying into the program of self-realization so I could grow into my truest nature as an imperfect, compassionate, human being.

I was embracing uncertainty, the unknown, anxiety, all my emotions, the truth, connecting to my darkness, transforming it.

I took the plunge into uncertainty and the unknown so I could open to becoming more and more of myself.

STOP; come here; LISTEN.
Stop; pay attention, TURN AROUND.
See all of you
Stop, WELCOME to my heart.
I AM finally HERE and present.

25

DIS-EASE

"The doctor I would want for myself or for anyone I cared about would be one who understands that disease is more than just a clinical entity; it is an experience and a metaphor, with a message that must be listened to."

-Bernie Siegel, MD

Chronic dis-ease has been a crucible into an initiation that brought me to an authentic, passionate life. Being ill at ease has been a challenge, a great and tough awakening — and it may have even saved my life. Persephone was kidnapped by Hades, the Greek God of the underworld and the dead. Persephone became the Goddess of the mysterious underworld. She was permitted to surface in the spring for half a year. This myth has several versions that explain the seasons of growth and flourishing and then barrenness.

Over and over, the manifestations of chronic dis-ease abducted me into hell. It has brought despair, fear, and awakening to my doorstep.

For the longest time, I didn't know when a feeling of "lack of ease and unwellness" would strike.

It was the summer of 1956. My grandparents had a summer home on Lake Shenarock, not too far from New York City. We would stay there for long periods of time.

There was a beach near the house where day after day, I played with my pail and shovel, joyfully running in and out of the water. Suddenly, seemingly out of nowhere, I was struck down by agonizing neck pain. I laid on the sliding glider couch on the screened-in porch surrounded by the trees, the melodies of birds, children playing in the distance and my family's conversations nearby. I was in hell and so far, away.

My parents and grandparents didn't know how to help me. My basic needs were always met, yet my suffering continued. No one understood the severity of what I had to endure. I rarely complained except when I couldn't move or was in excruciating pain.

They didn't know of any natural pain remedies and there was a great deal of unconsciousness and denial around my situation. It was tough for a little 18-month-old.

That said, when I take a moment and reflect on those times, the main ingredient that I experience is how much I was loved. So, yes, there was tension, dissonance, a lack of harmony in my body, my mind and my spirit and a great sense of love. Yet my ability to be resilient was remarkable.

An episode would surface, and I would be plummeted into the depths of hell and then miraculously, a few days later, I would return to a state of flourishing and optimal energy. The Persephone pattern, waking up in hell and then flourishing, plagued me throughout my childhood and into my young-adult years.

At first when I was in hell, I felt like I had been abducted from life. I was a helpless victim. The chronic dis-ease was an enemy, something I shouldn't have or something I needed to get rid of. So, I would tuck away my feelings into a tiny little pocket deep inside and every now and again I became aware of the ever-present and under-the-radar experience of something not being right.

For many years, I passed through the halls of a myriad of emotions, agitation, anger, terror, loneliness, betrayal, insecurity, confusion, and shame. I had no idea that emotional pain, physical pain, mental pain, and the spiritual life were connected in any way.

When I was a teenager, I started to make connections through journaling. First, I became aware of how much I judged and minimized myself. And then, I woke up to how I had tightly held false beliefs about myself, others, and the world.

I had a lot to learn.

Birth trauma, neck and back pain, gut issues, concussions, hormonal issues, emotional holding, chronic Lyme disease, co-infections, hearing loss, walking difficulties, food sensitivities, oh my!!

Chronic dis-ease initiated me into the world of deep mysteries. I clearly had to yield to Hades and wake up.

A lot of memory is subconscious, and gets stored throughout the body, mind, and spirit as cellular memory. It is amazing that the body can hold memories that are hidden outside of the brain. The stockpile of memories often affects muscles, cells, fluids, the fascia, the bones, and more.

In addition, recent research has shown that many of our memories and fears are transgenerational. They are passed down from our ancestors through the DNA to prepare and protect us from difficult circumstances. Again, there is something here about the love of our ancestors. Yet the survival patterns that are formed limit proper functioning.

My body and nervous system were very sensitive and easily activated by physical, emotional, and mental stress.

This lowered my immune system and wreaked havoc on my endocrine system.

Emotionally, I learned how to minimize and disconnect from all sorts of difficulties except when I had the painful episodes. Chronic dis-ease was my nemesis, I wanted to stay far away from it. I didn't want to relate to it. I wanted it to go away, far, far away. I was separate from myself.

Simultaneously, I experienced positive chemical benefits of being wrapped in a cocoon of love, and this was the foundation to my resilience. The chemicals that are elicited, oxytocin and dopamine, are both known to be "feel good" chemicals and may be responsible for a balanced sense of positive feelings.

As I realized on a very deep level that I couldn't change what happened in the past, but that I could change my relationship to it, I relaxed on all levels: body, mind, and soul.

Waking up through meditation and psychotherapy was fantastic. I connected my emotions with my pain. I became more conscious of my thoughts and my needs. I started to express myself more. Yet it wasn't enough.

Meditation helped me to be more present; and that wasn't enough.

Having a lifetime of unexplained episodes of dis-ease created my insatiable need to access information about natural healing and psychoneuroimmunology; mind-body science. I needed to expand my knowledge and access my inner wisdom. I read everything I could get my hands on in the pre-internet world and took workshops and post-graduate training in various therapeutic modalities, spiritual exploration, healing and awakening and an immersion into non-mainstream nutrition and wellness.

For whatever reason, chronic inflammation caused my body to think it was under constant attack. I was on a mission to find the root cause and move on. I wanted the $50-million answer as if there were a miracle cure that would solve all my problems and take away all my pain and make me immortal. Crazy, yes? Yes.

Looking for the root cause may be an interesting part of the journey. And then again, it may be like the play by Samuel Beckett, *Waiting for Godot*. Spoiler alert: Godot never arrives.

When I stopped looking for meaning and the answer to why, that helped calm me down. What I found was more of myself. I didn't always like what I found, yet I embodied more wholeness.

As I unraveled many of my false beliefs and preconceptions about myself, life, and everything, I focused on what I wanted to experience instead. I unwound the creaky old patterns and became willing to be in a deeper relationship with what was in the moment. I reorganized my whole self on every level. I became freer.

I realized that I needed to set my intention: how did I want to act and live with chronic dis-ease? I needed to get in touch and wrestle with what I wanted to change and how I wanted to access my wisdom. For example, I wanted to believe that I could live in harmony with life as it is. This included the idea that I was willing to live in harmony even with dissonances, with my physical conditions and my emotional sensitivity. That was a big one for me.

Having chronic dis-ease has been a constant growth opportunity for me. It took a huge commitment and a lot of courage to plow a path less traveled. I needed to discover what my limitations and blind spots were. I needed to pay attention to my longing to have access to my wisdom. I needed to open and grow. I needed to be patient and loving with myself.

As I acknowledged all the aspects of myself and gave them a place in my heart, I became more vulnerable, more open, more real, and more present. My inner wisdom spoke to me as I opened the curtain and paid attention.

After all, healing comes from within. I realized that I had a lot of needs and honoring those was a revelation.

I found that I needed more time for creativity, more time to explore without a goal, I needed to change my diet, I needed to pay more attention to my emotions and my thoughts along with my body's needs every day. I knew that I couldn't do the healing alone and I realized I needed support. That was a big deal.

The chronic dis-ease whether physical, mental, emotional, or spiritual, has been a portal into my true self and reality. When I embrace it all, I ride back on the curve that is my resilience and find courage, and strength.

Allowing myself to be where I am, even if it's a difficult place, allows me to be enveloped and held by love.

What I discovered in hell was a treasure. When I allowed myself to touch my suffering, I experienced more compassion.

Some days are good, and some days are tough. I embrace where I am as best as I can.

Chronic dis-ease had been an enemy and now I realize that it has been an accelerator of awakening and healing.

I have changed my lifestyle from one that was constantly filled with work to one that is more creative, spacious, and open to being in touch with life as it is.

As I have traversed my personal suffering and the love in my life, I am seated in more of my whole self. This has given me more ease and joy.

Pain, move, pain, breathe, pain, stretch, pain, drink, pain, eat, pain, love, pain, meditate, repeat.

My body is my temple.

26

CRACKING THE CODE

"Dancing along in the madness there is no sadness,
only the song of the soul."

~Chris Williamson

For many lifetimes, I locked parts of myself inside a secret, invisible vault. It took many iterations of transformation to crack the code. Once a year during the winter solstice, the light would beam onto the stone which protected it from being unearthed until ...

This time around, I had a good enough childhood. We lived with my grandparents for the first year or so of my life while my father built his professional career. There were the natural tensions with three working adults, one new mother and an infant in a small two-bedroom apartment in New York City.

I always knew and felt wanted and loved. That created an inner security in me even though I always experienced an underlying hidden feeling of discomfort.

There were guidelines about how to be a good little girl from as long ago as I can remember and probably from even before that. There were family norms, cultural norms, city-slicker norms and ancestral norms that I carried deep inside and that I had to fit into.

In my family in the 1950's New York City, girls were supposed to act, look, and be proper. They were to speak when spoken to, always be agreeable, and never color outside of the lines. That meant that I should not be demanding, not say too much and not be myself, somehow. Don't ask too many questions; you may appear stupid. Stay quiet and reserved and have your little hands in your lap and never ever spread your legs. That one never made sense when I was little.

Everyone wanted me to be a good and nice little girl, so I tucked parts of myself away so well they were hidden from me for a very long time.

I held my breath most of the time to make certain I was on the right track, acting in the prescribed manner. If there was any sign of disapproval, I would change my behavior midstream as it crushed my little heart and spirit.

And then I would tighten my body even more, so I created a rigidity and felt fear. My sense of constancy wavered. My spontaneity dissipated, I became controlled and hidden.

My parents were very artsy and creative and yet there was nothing about developing my imagination or being creative. I packed away my curiosity and spontaneity.

Can't a pig fly and a cow be yellow? Can't a dog be purple, and a house be crooked? Everything had to be just so — and boring. Blech.

As my ego and my sense of a separate self-developed, I had to split the world and myself to make sense of it all. This was good and that was bad. Focus on the outside and don't pay too much attention to the inside. This behavior received approval, and that behavior was rejected. There was always a right way and a wrong way.

Kindergarten should have been about developing friendships, strengthening self-esteem, learning the alphabet, learning how to cooperate with others, using curiosity for learning, investigating together, supporting our creativity, and having fun. But there were so many rules and regulations. For example, at a prescribed time, we had to have milk and cookies even if we weren't hungry and then we had to lie down and take a nap on a blanket on the floor even if we weren't tired. It was a bad babysitting service. Clearly, the program wasn't stimulating or child centric.

First grade wasn't much better. Thankfully, there was a lot more creative learning, better teachers, and engagement in school once I was in second grade.

I did all the things that a good little girl would do. My homework was always done in a timely fashion, my room was always organized, my clothing was clean. I learned to smile even when I wasn't happy, I was quiet even when I wanted to be loud and run around, be ridiculous and have fun just because.

A protective invisible shell grew around me, I needed to be shielded to get through each day. Often, I didn't know how to be. I wanted to be seen as a good, smart, and talented girl, so I worked hard to be one. I needed a step-by-step guidebook telling me how to be good, smart, and talented for each age.

My fear of being judged in any way stopped me in my tracks. I wanted to ask questions but wouldn't dare take the chance of being judged. My fear was that I would be ridiculed in front of the class like some of the other kids had been and I wasn't going to ever risk having that happen.

My mission was to receive love, approval and to be adored at all costs. The price was that I lost my dynamic self and my vitality. Mission accomplished.

Until my preteen years, I lived in a box, hidden from my inner light; I was successful at being a very good girl, I knew just how to be, what to do and how to excel in school. Living in my box, I learned how to contain myself and split away from the discomfort of any dissonances of any kind. I was a pro at splitting away from my emotions and needs.

And then my hormones rushed in.

As a teenager, I broke out of the box. I refused to live a phony, masked, game-playing, illusion of myself.

It was essential that I escape from the tight, secretive protective box of my formative years. It kept me safe; it helped me survive and yet I was twisted and bound. My natural innate life force and rhythm called to me to wake up. I was no longer able to or willing to live split and disconnected.

So as many teenagers and young adults do, I started to express myself and not hold back. My parents were the main objects of my outrage. I thought that was freedom. I was not elegant or polished. I wanted to run wild in the streets. And I still wanted to save the world. I put my passions into my studies.

As I cracked the code, I slowly and with great hesitation opened the hidden vault of truth. I had no idea what I would find inside.

It finally made sense; for forever and a day I had believed that I was bad and didn't deserve love. On a very deep level I had been affected by these beliefs all along but when it wasn't conscious, I was able to ignore the suffering that it caused me.

With a bright flash of light, I realized I had been all the things I abhorred in others. I was judgmental, angry, hateful, manipulative, arrogant, and grandiose. I had no idea how to live with these truths. I was at a loss. This was the treasure that I hid from myself so that once I was safe to uncover it became my foundation for healing.

However, for many years, I still lived split apart since once I knew that I was flawed, I carried my shame in my heart. This way, I was able to hide, deny, and keep secret any flaws. I pretended "as if" I were fine and robotically went through life. And I did that so well. But I was oh so lonely.

There was the part of me that was caring, fearful, and a good soul. And then there was the angry, wild, vibrant, and creative not-so-good young woman who wanted to feel the wind, taste the sun, dig into the earth, roll around and be free and natural.

One day I woke up and I was a rebel. My energy erupted and I needed to let it all out, I couldn't keep myself hidden any longer. I thought I was omnipotent and that I knew everything, those adults were just the walking dead.

I was a whirlwind, I left messy towns behind me. I thought if you feel it, let it out, it was good, I didn't consider whether I would hurt others, I didn't really care. I had no skillful means at all. Anger, judgment, premature sexual activity, manipulation and more.

And little did I know that the hurt and suffering was still inside of me. I was just acting it out to feel better.

One of my issues, that I worked on for a long time, was my concern about what others thought about me. This really plagued me. Simultaneously, I was on the path to waking up and becoming more real and compassionate because I was more and more honest with myself than ever before.

Diving into a philosophical and contemplative journey to become my truest self, along with some political activism, really helped me in the early 70's. It gave me a place and a purpose. I felt connected with many liberally minded people who wanted to awaken and change the world.

As I woke up and walked on a healing and awakening path, I learned how to honestly express myself from my heart. I settled down and felt more aligned with what was my natural self.

Longing to be whole and dance to my own rhythm, I engaged in many pursuits of consciousness-raising. As I developed the courage to be myself and pay impeccable attention to my needs, I took one step, then another, so that I could transform the beliefs that kept me tight and hidden.

Decades later, and with a lot of healing and life lived, I have opened to the vitality and compassion embedded in being all of who I am and why I am here.

27

IMPERFECTION

"The more I feel imperfect, the more I feel alive."

-Jhumpa Lahiri

What in the world ever made me think that "perfection" was the absolute goal? Why would that be my pursuit of happiness? And why would I pursue an impossible task?

The irony of it all is that there's imperfection everywhere we look! A crack here, a blemish there, something is flawed, confusion, illusion, and delusion. I was self-critical and constantly compared myself to others. How sad and crazy was that?

Little did I know at the time, I had a deep inner conflict-I thought that I should be different from how I was, how I looked, how I spoke, and not have my own ideas and thoughts. I believed I was expected to be a certain way that I interpreted as being in the image of something and someone else. I believed that there was danger in being myself and that I wouldn't receive the love and appreciation that I craved.

Striving to reach the impossible goal of perfection was rooted in my feelings of an overall sense of inadequacy and insecurity. In addition, there was the confusion about my body image. The teen and fashion magazines of the time displayed body types that I measured myself against. Many of the movie stars and cover girls of those times had emaciated bodies or were stunningly beautiful. I compared myself to the ideal, I criticized myself and I felt like a failure. Clearly, I was worshipping the wrong things.

As a young adult, I became more focused on the imperfections of the world and my desire to save it. I became immersed in my studies, mostly psychology, anthropology, and spiritual growth. My training in counseling and making a difference for others was deeply rewarding and fulfilling. I was focused on something fundamentally important; I was doing something that helped others and in turn helped me in my personal healing. I had found my calling.

Psychologically and spiritually, my self-esteem was strengthened, and my body image became balanced. I no longer compared myself to cover girls or beauty queens. I was much more satisfied, fulfilled, and subsequently happier.

And ... beneath my social and educational successes, I still was on the perfection trail.

As I experimented with various spiritual and meditation groups, I decided I needed to exile my ego and my emotions. That seemed to be the best path, reclaim your ego after having lost it and then rid self and become merged in the oneness of reality. What could be better than that?

Well, it didn't work. Something just didn't feel right. After all, I am a human being and I live in this world, I had way too may reactions to situations, internally I was turbulent, and I wanted to be of this world. My mission of finding perfection started to transform ever so slowly. Ugh, I had a lot more healing to do.

On the next part of my journey, I focused on the physical. As I became more aware of the sensations in my body, there was a growing sense of toxicity. It appeared to be physical, so I thought I needed to purify myself of any toxicity whatsoever. I set out on a journey to perfect my body.

Asceticism is the denial of physical or psychological desires to reach a goal. Over the centuries most religions have had sects that included various forms of asceticism, I figured why not, maybe it will work.

What I discovered was a whole world of detoxification, I was excited; maybe I would reach perfection through purification. It was worth trying. I started with a water fast once a week, I realized I was a failure as an ascetic because I was only able to do the water fasting a few times. The feeling of deprivation wasn't for me. Then I learned about juice fasting, that was easier, felt better and was a whole lot better.

I figured if I was going to purify my body, I should feel good in the process. If I could purify out the toxins, I would be more perfect, more spiritual, more awake, more enlightened, more this and more that. All to reach the top rung of the ladder where I could grab the gold ring, it would be mine and finally arrive.

Little did I know, I was avoiding a true connection with myself. I was avoiding my suffering and my deepest longing, to be whole. I was taking detours I thought were good for me, but I was mistaken. I wasn't aware at all of the stress that I was creating internally by engaging with my goal of attempting to attain the impossible.

I was missing out on living and all of life's nuances. I didn't get to appreciate the natural beauty of imperfection. And yet, I truly yearned to find what could support me on a deep level to be whole, seated in myself, and present.

Searching for perfection took me away from my truest self. I was on a train without brakes and was heading for danger. Simultaneously, everything I tried and did led me to discover more of my awakening self.

I stepped off the limiting perfection train and onto the imperfection road, which is so much more spacious and less stressful. I began to see the beauty in imperfection. I developed a relationship with all the vulnerable parts of myself and with my strengths.

I committed to connecting my mind, body, heart, and spirit as I took a deep dive into the story of my history and my ancestors. I surrendered to the truth which is, I am an imperfect person, and I am willing to be honest and vulnerable about that. I needed to realize that chasing the perfection rainbow was a deterrent from being real. I longed to be comfortable in my skin and in my body.

In the beginning there was fear, hesitation, shame, and hope. My goal was to become a compassionate person, mother, wife, friend, therapist. The whole arc and shape of my being changed, I became right side up.

And I realized my courage to deeply touch the truth. Through meditation, following my heart, accepting the errors of my ways, opening to receiving messages from my failures and all the difficulties I encountered along the way, I learned and felt how much resilience I had developed over the years.

As I held the imperfections from my history and the present day as close as close could be, I created a home for my suffering in my heart. I stopped rejecting myself.

And then I went deeper. I connected with the truth that life itself is imperfect. Life is impermanent. We are born, we live for a time, some of us will get ill and all of us will die.

I created a more spacious container within myself. Now, I can ride the waves of the difficulties and the preciousness of life. There is space for all of me and all of life in my mind, my body, my heart, and my spirit.

My prayer is that realizing the truth of my humanity and embodying all of who I am will lead me to more skillful means. Even though I falter at times, my intention is to deliver teachings and messages in a compassionate, effective manner and to always appreciate our individual differences.

The aging lines on my face, loving, the grey in my hair, caring, the pain in my body, receiving, sleepless nights, blessing, making mistakes, honesty, forgetting and always remembering that *"life's a journey and not a destination."*

There is always some sort of imperfection, no matter what. There is beauty within imperfection if we have the heart to realize it. It took me years of traveling through life, being with my suffering, my joy, my grief, and my love to discover the beauty of it all.

I keep awakening and healing.

28

POWER

"Power to the people, power to the people,
power to the people, power to the people right on.
You say you want a revolution...."

~John Lennon

The music of the '60s and early '70s brought a deep feeling of connection and belonging to me. Rock and rollers and folk singers were insistent about the fight for equality, justice, and societal change. The music and the lyrics resonated with me on a very deep level; they expressed what I couldn't concretize. Each time I turned on the radio or played an album, it reminded me of the truth—I was not alone.

The song "*Power to the People*," by John Lennon, was both empowering and confusing for me. I longed for change, and I was up for protesting. Yet, I wasn't interested in being a part of a revolution or being militant in any way. I believed that there had to be a more empowered and compassionate way to heal myself and the world.

At that time, I was still quite young, and immature and I didn't know how to own my power or what having power even meant. I just knew that I often felt powerless. There was something missing and distorted inside of me. And I didn't know what it was.

The origin of the word *power* is a Latin derivative, *posse* or *potere*, meaning to be able. In Greek, power means potential or ability. So, what if power is about mobilizing and taking action? I knew I could do that, so that was good. My desire to be an agent of change solidified my hunger for discovering true power.

There are so many types of power. There's personal power, physical power, power in leadership, political power, to name a few of the ways in which we experience power.

We hear about the abuse and distortion of power all the time. Manipulation by executives, bullying, exploitation by politicians, sexual assault, coercive behavior, and domination over those in lesser positions are a few of the ways we see an unevolved form of power acted out. This lack of consciousness about power often leads to the breakdown of relationships of all sorts.

To be a conscious and empowered leader, I needed to take a good look at myself, I needed to discover and uncover what was hidden and keeping me stuck. I knew deep in my heart that how I thought I should be, act, look and express myself was a result of the limitations of my family and culture, and ultimately my fear of being honest and authentic.

As a young girl, I gave my power away. I sequestered any signs of what might have been deemed negative. Mostly I feared disapproval and the withdrawal of love. There was nothing worse than that. I became obedient, good-natured, and respectful.

My school dress code didn't allow girls to wear pants until we were in eighth grade. And those stockings with those garter belts that we had to use to hold them up, talk about discomfort! The rules for girls were different than for boys and clearly not based on what would be best for our personal growth.

Since I was repressed, I experienced a fragility that I believed I needed to protect. I wasn't visible, I rarely said what was on my mind, and I kept my feelings and thoughts buried. This often left me sad, lonely, and angry.

As a teenager, I believed that power was either something that you gave up or something that you abused. It was one way or the other. So, I was either powerless or powerful, or, a victim or a perpetrator. Much of my powerlessness was fear-based and was derived from the belief that the world was unsafe and that I was unsafe because I could be harmed or cause harm. What a dilemma.

One of my routes to disempowerment was embedded in my belief that I had to be a certain way to be accepted. Historically, in my lineage and the western culture, girls and women were not to have any power and if we showed any sign of power we were thought of as whores or burned at the stake. I certainly didn't want people to think of me in that way.

Our culture taught me that powerful women were domineering, pushy and demanding bitches. That was not what I aspired to be. This stopped me from fully being who I was. I was frustrated.

Other messages I received from the environment that I grew up in were that girls and women should know their place, act in a particular way, dress a certain way, and behave themselves by doing what they were told. And women shouldn't look or act like men or even do the same type of things that men do.

It seems to me that the message perpetrated in our society was to keep women in subservient positions.

Since I wasn't in an honest relationship with myself, I was reactive and lived in fear. Acting out and being reactive was not empowerment. It was the misuse of power. It didn't heal my inner demons; in fact, it perpetuated them. I was unconscious and stuck.

Also, even though I was an athletic and physically strong young woman, I always feared being in a situation where I could be overpowered by a man and not able to protect or defend myself. I was one of the fortunate ones. Internationally, one in three girls and women have suffered from some type of sexual violation in their lifetime.

As I matured and became more conscious, becoming empowered became an ever present thought in my life. My desire to be myself—a natural, empowered young woman grew stronger and stronger.

As I pursued the world of personal growth, I realized that my focus on being and feeling safe had been my primary concern.

When I had something controversial to say, the sense of danger lurked inside of me. I shielded myself by avoiding certain positions and contentious conversations for a long time. As I matured and became more courageous and honest with myself, I owned that it was much easier to blame others then to take responsibility for my actions.

The more I longed to be the woman that I was born to be, the more I opened my heart to the truth of how I acted and how I was ready to become my true self. I wanted a map with very specific instructions about how to be empowered.

The women's movement was inspiring. Incredible women such as Gloria Steinem and Shirley Chisolm were breaking down barriers and opening up opportunities for girls and women.

Bella Abzug was a Jewish American lawyer, a U.S. Representative, a social activist, and a leader in the women's movement. She was a powerhouse.

Her nickname was "Battling Bella." Even if she was upset by what people thought of her, her mission was never compromised. Bella didn't let fear get in her way. She was completely devoted to pushing into the world of women's rights. She made a difference; her powerful words were imprinted on my heart and mind. One thing she espoused was, *"A women's place is in the house — the House of Representatives."* Yay!

Betty Frieden, also a Jewish woman, was the cofounder of the National Organization for Women; she used her power and focused on equality for women. She supported and advocated for the Equal Rights Amendment and was active in supporting the positive changes in the abortion laws. We could use her now, that's for sure.

The empowerment of the *9-to-5 movement* gave woman more rights in the work force even though there were still sexual injustices in the late 70's as there are today. All those women opposed the status quo; they were determined, courageous, and persistent. They changed the work culture from their refusal to back down even though many lost their jobs and had to rebuild their livelihoods. They didn't let fear get in their way and they were supported by a large nationwide community of women and political activists.

Feminism and the demonstration of women's power and the fight for gender equality calmed and inspired me. Do you know that the Equal Right's Amendment, hasn't been ratified after all these years? I find that astounding. And meanwhile, right now in 2023, there are many states taking away the reproductive rights of women. How disturbing.

"Fight for the things that you care about but do it in a way that will lead others to join you." Ruth Bader Ginsburg was a Jewish, married mother and was most well known as the second woman to be a Supreme Court justice. She successfully fought against gender discrimination and pay inequality.

Her personal struggles did not stop her from pursuing her passion, getting her law degree while being married and having children, and fighting for what she knew was essential for human rights. She confronted many barriers because she was a woman and simultaneously, she used her power to create change.

Since I longed to wake up and be a compassionate and powerful woman—not an acting out obnoxious woman, I knew that I had to shine a light on what I was doing, how I was acting, and what I was feeling.

Raising my consciousness was essential. Connecting to and owning the various parts of myself made a huge difference in my ability to be a responsible and heart centered woman.

First, I took full responsibility for my actions and developed relationships with the various parts of myself. There was the part that felt safer being powerless and the part that wanted to act out by being power hungry. And then there was the part that judged others, the part that was jealous, the part that was self-critical, the part that hated, the part that loved and then there were my vulnerable parts.

When I had a difficult communication of some sort, I was often triggered into unhealed emotional turmoil from my history. It took a lot of inner work and awareness about my reactivity to be able to be in true, intimate relationships with others.

It took courage to touch and experience my vulnerability. This made a huge difference in my embodiment of true power.

For way too long, I avoided the anxiety and the beauty of being seen. When I was ready, I strengthened my commitment to expressing my full potential in this life. In my fear I was powerless. When I took action, I felt empowered, and I promoted healing and transformation for others.

As I stepped into my true power, I took a bunch of actions.

Focusing on my studies, getting help, meditating, practicing yoga, socializing, reading, listening to music, travelling, volunteering — all empowered me.

There was deep personal power and profound healing embedded in giving my confusions, distortions, and illusions a place in my mind, body, and spirit, of remembering my history, acknowledging the suffering of my lineage, and of sharing my story.

I met with trustworthy people so that they could remind me of my blind spots and offer me support. I admitted to having difficulties and allowed each piece to have a home in my heart even when it was painful.

I went beyond my fears and included my fears; I stopped focusing on what others might think, say, or feel about me. I focused on my needs and desires and the needs and desires of my loved ones and clients.

As I honestly allowed each part of me to touch my heart, be acknowledged, and allowed to exist, I became more and more whole and truly powerful.

I accepted that I am imperfect and that I may hurt myself and others, even though I don't want to. I no longer stop the flow of my life force. I am engaged with life. And I bring all of life into my heart and allow wisdom to flow.

By allowing vulnerability without having to dominate myself or others I continue to develop my compassionate open heart toward life.

When I'm honest and allow myself to have a true relationship with my powerful and powerless parts, I am liberated. Today, I am empowered and courageous most of the time.

29

SURRENDER

"Try something different — surrender."

~Rumi

For eons, I scattered myself throughout the universe. Preparing my body, mind, heart, and spirit for true surrender took lots of tumbling through the world to retrieve the fragments of my soul.

Over the years people said, "Just let go." That's easier said than done, I couldn't just let go until I could!

Once I realized that surrender is not resignation, it's not submission, it can't be forced, it's a natural awakening and when the conditions are aligned with the stars, the heart, and the cosmos, there can be an organic opening into the portal of true surrender.

Receiving my deeper wisdom allowed me to honor my pace and from there, well, it has been a natural transformation. It was a foreign territory filled with emptiness, fullness, and uncertainty.

SURRENDER

I am losing my grasp,
one side or the other flailing.

Where is comfort? Certainty?

My broken heart
beyond the false appearances and shadows.
Here now.

Holding on to Fantasy.
Where are the strongholds? Were there ever any?

Now,
Surrender is my homeland.

So, here's my little story about returning home.

I was completely and utterly attached to what I deemed was the correct path in life. My heart may have been defended but I figured I was safe enough and feeling safe was my goal for a very long time, until I realized the truth about safety.

My inner false authority believed that my preconceptions about life and my tattered understanding about how I should be, act and live, how others should be, act and live, and how the world should be were based in truth and reality.

My mission was to avoid the reality of my broken heart.

Safety wasn't something that I could acquire or buy at Neiman Marcus or Bergdorf's! I chiseled away until I realized that's not how to arrive in the land of surrender, true safety was being in relationship with all of who I am, period. Like it or not.

Grief, hurt, dissatisfaction, confusion, questioning, grasping, and control. I didn't want to feel defeated and yet I needed to pass through the land of defeat and resignation. I didn't want to feel shame and yet I needed to visit the horror of shame and the desert's loud silence in which I resided for decades.

Longing to be free, I tried to get rid of all my personal suffering. I wanted something else instead of being in relationship with what was.

For decades and probably lifetimes, I prayed to be blessed by the shimmering light of reality. I filled my backpack with water and granola, some photos of my loves and put on those old Timberland hiking boots.

With my wooden oars and clumsiness, I gently entered my canoe — hook, line, and sinker! There was no turning back on the precipice of my soul's retrieval.

And by the way, I had no idea that I needed to traverse the deep, dark, cold, desert. I spent years specializing in understanding how I got to where I was, I connected to my childhood, I connected to the imperfections of myself, my family, and life itself.

I needed to know more of who I was before I could let go and surrender, otherwise there would be a complete separation between my heart and my soul. I wanted to be integrated and not split off into the realm of unicorns and fairy tales.

Meditation, yoga, psychotherapy, healing, praying, spiritual healing, bodywork, energy psychology, imagery, plant medicine, reading, questing, kinesiology, herbs, mother-ing, wife-ing, daughtering, sistering, aunting, rescuing four-leggeds, journaling, traveling, healing the inner child, birthing, deathing...my human life.

All of that said, it's not easy to surrender and let go. I was terrified. Who would I be if I truly surrendered? Would I have to give up the territory I had fought so hard to claim as mine and devoted my life to? Would I be seen as a fool?

After about 10 years downstream I saw that surrender was not about becoming resigned to another's will. I realized that what was next was my need to unravel the cords that kept me bound and paralyzed for lifetimes.

Around the bend about 5 years further in, there was a lean-to where I rested for a while, sort of like on the Appalachian Trail. As I lay in the sun, the birds all around me with the pines and the hydrangea and the noises of the townies nearby, in my open-hearted access to other dimensions, I saw a golden castle! This place of beauty and refuge entered me as I entered it.

I was ready to name my shame as I basked in the golden threads of my soul's guidance. Here, I was held and ready to completely own my transgressions, I remembered and touched the wounds of my history, my pain, grief, sorrow, anger, desires, hurts and dreams.

I kept diving deeper and deeper, year after year, breaststroke after breaststroke, breath after breath. I saw, felt, and heard, all my connections, *"mitakuye oyasin"*—the Lakota people's expression for the interconnectedness of their people—and all my loves through all this life and probably beyond filling my heart. I knew I was and am not alone.

As I walked the maze at Grace Cathedral in San Francisco, I knew it was time. Now, I can let go and surrender.

All my vulnerabilities lined up before me, they had been waiting for this moment to return home, home to my heart. I expressed my gratitude and I allowed myself to know my courage and not dismiss it, maybe for the first time.

The tabooed parts, the beautiful parts, the ugly, the silent, the hidden, the funny, the bright, the resilient, and the shy, welcome home. So much of me was kept separate to protect me; the more I healed, the more I reclaimed the missing hidden parts. The most exciting part was the return of my creativity, joy, and true unadulterated love — just ask my husband, son, and grandson and a few of my clients and students too!

Thinking that I had to be free of negativity was the opposite of what I needed to do. I needed to include all parts of myself including the parts that were sequestered because as a child they wouldn't be approved of. I may not approve of my thoughts or feelings, but I included them because I knew I would feel more whole.

What was really a relief, and a miracle was that I didn't have to recover every part of myself to feel whole. We just need enough of the parts of ourselves to make the quantum leap and feel whole and still accept our imperfection.

I welcomed all my thoughts and I no longer wanted to stamp them out. Heart opening, body settling, natural, original, real, honest, and true.

Exhausted from holding on and trying to control myself, others, and life, I breathed, let go, fell back into the fullness of emptiness.

Intention, commitment to being of service to the world, surrendering arrived naturally when I exhausted myself emotionally, mentally, and spiritually. Then and only then was I able to let go.

I gathered my threads together into my heart and swam back up to the surface, went back to my canoe and went to the pick-up station where my husband drove us home.

The original me was birthed in those waters. My essence was glowing.

Now I can be with each arising. I can hold it close and allow it to naturally become itself.

Dedication, commitment, and intention are my sisters.

30

MYSTERY

*"There is nothing in a caterpillar that
tells you it's going to be a butterfly."*

~R. Buckminster Fuller

Mystery whispered. "Come here, pay attention, listen, open your eyes, smell, touch. And most of all, question everything."

The magnetic secrets of mystery attracted me like filings toward the positive node. I longed to understand and discover that which is hidden from us and yet still exists and affects us on fundamental levels.

As a child, I loved mathematics and playing with numbers, especially those mathematical word problems. They would break my mind open and use my brain to solve something that wasn't explicit. It was so stimulating and enriching. Math was transformational for me.

Discovering the amazing wisdom of the Fibonacci sequence, a series of numbers where each number is the sum of the preceding two numbers, made so much sense to me. It is also known as nature's secret code. It's found in the petals of sunflowers and roses, on the spirals of pinecones, and on starfish. Part of what's awesome is that I was always attracted to these specific flowers, pinecones, and starfish. Who knew?!

At night, I laid in bed, the room darkened, the shades drawn, the door shut, my eyes closed, and my dog cuddled next to me. In my mind, I played with numbers for hours, reaching to touch infinity. For some reason, I imagined that in that velvety darkness, if I pushed out far enough with mathematical equations, infinity — the mystery of the cosmos — would surround me.

Usually, I arrived at a billowy cloudlike darkness, I would touch it, be comforted by it and then I would sleep. And I slept really well back in those days.

Life is shrouded in mystery. There are so many concealed and hidden dimensions. This is where religion, philosophy, science, mathematics, art, and psychology emerge from and ask the questions that humankind has contemplated about reality, all trying to make sense and express the beauty of the great unknown.

Probing into the mysteries of inner space was my heart's desire. I remember sitting on the floor in my bedroom immersing myself in sci-fi magazines. I religiously watched *The Outer Limits, The Twilight Zone*, Hitchcock, *Lost in Space*, and the original *Star Trek*; they were gifts that helped to broaden my exploration of the unknown mystery of life.

By the way, I was also a girl who loved to be of this everyday ordinary world too. I played sports, went to summer camp, dated, read *Archie* and *Veronica* comics and of course I gazed at the stars at night as my friends and I contemplated the purpose of it all.

In 1968, *Planet of the Apes* and *2001: A Space Odyssey* were on the big screen in the theatres. They were in alignment with my philosophy of "question everything." They opened me up to so many things in a brilliant and creative way, what has been (racism), what could be, (apocalypse), and what might need to be.

Did you know there are at least a hundred billion galaxies out there? Isn't that incredible? And on this website, (https://www.space.com/) they discuss the limitations of the present-day technology, leaving the estimates of galaxies between 100 billion and 200 billion. Just that in and of itself takes us into the reaches of the deepest unknowns on the physical level.

Our world as we know it, even our universe, is just a small facet of the glorious jewel of creation.

Spring was often the time of year when I planted flowers or vegetables around the perimeter of my childhood home. As I dug into the earth, I would pause because I was awestruck to watch the earthworms and the teeny creatures scurry about. The earth was cold, fertile, rich, and so alive. There was a whole world in the ground just beneath where I walked each day.

It was so natural for me to feel the earth pull me toward it, and it was much more than a gravitational pull. Hiking and backpacking kept me deeply connected to the land. I even went winter backpacking and woke up to snow! I felt like I had been a medicine woman in a past life, not that I knew anything about past lives at that time. Hiking and camping helped me to be extremely present with each step and every breath. There was something magical and mystical even though it was the most natural thing to do and be.

My exploration of plant medicine began with psilocybin (magic mushrooms) in the early 1970's. Journeying with them seemed magical because they shifted my biochemistry into a more natural state of being and simultaneously opened the doors of perception to more of the dimensions of reality. And it made a difference for me. I touched the unknown mystery in a primal way by ingesting a vegetable.

Through the years my study and use of herbs and essential oils have brought me into a deeper relationship with the innate intelligence of plants, trees, soil, and of course mushrooms. Plant medicine is in harmony with life and nature. It is healing, it strengthens us and brings a vibrancy and wholeness into our bodies-minds-spirits.

It is said that every remedy for the ills of humankind can be found in the rainforest. Sadly, the rainforests have not been protected and according to the research of Harvard biologist Edward O. Wilson, many species of plants and animals are becoming extinct daily.

There is a symbiotic type of relationship with plants; they provide the oxygen we need for breathing and we help the plants to breathe with the carbon dioxide we exhale. It's a beautiful example of profoundly intimate relationship, we breathe each other, and we need each other.

During the first year after my mother passed, she appeared in many of my dreams. They were often predictive or visitation dreams. In one dream, we were driving on a winding hillside road on our way to lunch, it reminded me of roads in Europe. As I was turning on the curvy road to the left, I said, "*Mom, can you tell me what it was like to die?*" Her reply was, "*You will find out.*" I continued driving to the lovely restaurant in the country where she received a phone call. She took out her cell phone and briefly spoke. I asked who it was, and she replied, "*God.*" As simple as that.

Having mystical experiences changed my life, for the better. They helped me to reclaim more of the wholeness of who I am. Even though mystical experiences have been disregarded by some scientific researchers because of neurological explanations for many of the experiences, the healing that was embedded in these experiences made me more compassionate and authentic.

When I first began to explore mysticism, I bought books by famous scholars. *The Thirteen Petalled Rose* by Adin Steinsaltz, *Kabbalah* by Gerson Scholem and of course, *The Zohar.* (There is controversy around who the author is.)

As I delved into these books, I couldn't wrap my head or heart around what was being said. Clearly, there was a gate into the mysteries, and I was locked out. I tried reading out loud, but that didn't work. So, I put the books down for about a year. The key to the gate found me as I personally transformed and became more whole in heart, mind, and spirit. As I immersed myself in spiritual practices I experienced shifting patterns, more consciousness of obfuscations, and the experience of the Presence in my body, mind, heart, and spirit.

Spiritual practices opened me to a moment-to-moment appreciation of the unified consciousness that holds all of creation together in a type of network filled with light, darkness, shapes, patterns, and potentiality. Indra's net and jewels is the best description of what I experienced. It is a Sanskrit word that describes a net that stretches out in infinite dimensions and has jewels shimmering throughout creation. Buddhism teaches us that all phenomena co-arise and don't have independent origin.

Shamans and mystics from all religions and philosophies know this place. Every tradition has a creation story trying to make sense of it all.

What I have discovered is that my relationship with the mystery of life slowly unfolded, day by day, and no faster than that. There aren't any short cuts.

The Heart Sutra, also known in Buddhism as the *heart of the perfection of wisdom*, teaches us that emptiness is the nature of reality. It cuts through the illusions and delusions about life as it breaks apart our beliefs of everything. Nothing, absolutely nothing, exists as it appears.

Following the trail of mystery has been my occupation for most of my life. Curiosity, openness to reality, seeing the truth — and not always liking what I see. It has created a life of more spaciousness and the ability to be with the unknown most of the time.

When I start a session with a client, I don't have an agenda, I don't know where we are going. What I do know is that I am present, and I show up with whatever arises even when it is in difficult territory. Then we travel together on the wings of the unknown. It is a mysterious and intimate process that unfolds moment by moment. Curiosity and uncertainty are my companions. A feeling, a thought, or an image may arise in my consciousness, and we explore that. The sessions are deeply healing, even when there is a great deal of suffering.

Mystery carries me to her doorstep, across the threshold and into the realms of truth and reality. Paying attention to the gradual unfolding of each moment, I listen with my whole being. My eyes perceive the depths of what is in front of me. As I touch the earth below me and feel the dimensions of life all around me, the doors of perception open. And the scent of the aroma guides me home to my heart.

Life itself is a mystery. It includes pain, suffering, joy, love, art, music, and all dimensions of creativity. What a blessing.

31

KINDNESS

*"A single act of kindness throws out roots in all directions,
and the roots spring up and make new trees."*

~Amelia Earhart

From a young age, I have had a profound connection to
and relationship with the Holocaust. I was compelled
to read every book and watch as many documentaries
about the atrocities and horror of it all. I longed to be of
service in some way.

Most of the men that I dated before meeting my husband were children of survivors of the Holocaust. The
transgenerational effect is startling and is part of the collective unconscious that affects all of us. There has been a
great deal of research about the transgenerational effects of
the Holocaust and the inherited effects of the trauma of our
ancestors (see references section).

In the early 1980's, I volunteered to do research about
some of the effects of the Holocaust on the children of survivors (also known as Second Generation). I also interviewed
non-Jews who rescued Jews during the war.

This experience changed me. It was a crisp, spring Sunday morning as we drove from our tiny apartment on Manhattan's east side to Queens. My husband stayed in the car nearby as I met with a man who rescued Jews during WWII. He decided to join the Nazi party, even though he morally disagreed with everything the Nazi party represented. He felt it was safer to pledge his allegiance to the Nazi party and participate in various assignments to protect himself, his family, and those he rescued.

He was so excited to speak about his story with me, he stood up and shared story after story for several hours. I barely remember having to ask him any questions. It was as if he never had spoken about what he had been through. It was an honor to witness his courage and kindness. Not only did he need me to listen to his memories and experiences, but he needed to tell me about his hatred of the Nazi's and all they represented.

With disgust he showed me several artifacts with Nazi emblems embedded in them. I trembled from the horror of it all. This man hid Jews in his home because he believed it was the right thing to do. Understandably, he was outraged when he talked about those he had grown up with who participated in the atrocities against humanity.

Others that I interviewed said things such as they couldn't live with themselves if they had not disobeyed the authorities. There are documentaries showing how Nazi officers defied their sworn obedience and safely harbored Jews. Most of the people who were rescuers were ordinary citizens in the various European countries. I don't think their passion to rescue people was about being altruistic, but rescuing was a way to take action that aligned with their hearts, minds, and souls.

Miep Gies was a Dutch woman living and working in the Netherlands. She rescued and hid Anne Frank, her family and four other Jews in the secret annex behind the bookshelves above Otto Frank's business on the Prisengracht in Amsterdam. Once the Franks were betrayed and sent to the concentration camp, Miep found and kept Anne's diary until after the war, when she gave it to Otto Frank, the sole survivor of the family. Miep believed that rescuing and hiding eight people in the secret annex was her job as a human. Her remarkable compassion and integrity were expressed in her belief that, *"my story is a story of very ordinary people during extraordinarily terrible times."*

These huge acts of kindness are truly awe-inspiring.

True kindness is a natural state of being. It is so much more than being sympathetic or helpful. It is more than being generous. And so much more than being gentle, affectionate, and empathic.

We may never act as these people have. As ordinary people, though, I believe we can incorporate kindness into our lives each day and make a difference.

In Buddhism, a bodhisattva is a person who is able to reach nirvana, the liberation from suffering, and out of compassion chooses to devote their lives to freeing those who are suffering. When you are in relationship with your authentic imperfect human self and not separate from it, then you are naturally human and kind beings.

When we are in relationship with our suffering, we can be kind to others and take in and appreciate their suffering. In Judaism, it is taught that by showing kindness, we can help to heal the world. In the *Pirkei Avot*, a compilation of ethics, in Chapter 1:2, it teaches us *"by three things the world exists: On the Torah (the five books of Moses), on worship, and on acts of loving kindness."*

Healing into true kindness is counterintuitive. When we walk directly into and develop a relationship with the places that were prohibited and when we look deeply into the nature of our personal suffering, we unearth true compassion. We do this because we know that as we include our suffering, we develop a fabric woven from true inner kindness that is manna for our human condition.

Throughout my life, I always thought of myself as being kind and generous. For the first 30 years, I didn't realize that what was going on inside of me affected how others felt around me. I believed that if I turned "negative" emotions and reactions toward myself, then only I would be hurt. I couldn't have been more incorrect.

As I engaged with deep healing and awakening, I began to realize that my self-hatred, judgments and anger and other unhealed states of consciousness were infiltrating my expressions of kindness. When I was unkind to myself, then I could not have been fully embodying true kindness. Those learned behaviors and distorted belief systems stopped the organic movement of my life and my creativity.

For many years, I worked hard at rising above my animosity, ill will, hostility, and intolerance. By becoming conscious of how these patterns were a part of me, then and only then was I able to bring true kindness and true compassion into my heart. I transformed them through owning them and realizing the roots of my suffering.

As I became more and more aware of the destructive thoughts and feelings that I harbored toward myself and others, I learned how to hold those feelings with a kind and compassionate heart toward myself. As I allowed things to be what they were and to be present with them, I became deeply touched by kindness, I felt as if I was being held by the great mother, the loving source of all.

I knew that another type of generosity of my heart of hearts would be expressed as I seriously and honestly allowed myself to be in relationship with all of who I was and heal through the transformation of my wounds and the false beliefs that accompanied them.

In the psychology world, we talk about projected objects, the things that we don't want to own as ours, and thus, project onto other people. For example, if I feel angry and deny it, I could make it about the other person.

As a psychotherapist and healer, when I am sitting with someone, I can experience, feel, and see what someone isn't owning and what they are projecting outside of themselves. When we don't want to own our anger, arrogance, resentment, antagonism, judgments or anything that may be thought of as negative, it is still a part of us, it is actually in our energy field, and it effects all of our relationships. If we are willing to become aware of it, we can begin to experience ourselves as more authentic and whole.

When these unowned parts of ourselves are no longer kept separate and when we are more integrated, something else begins to happen; there is intimacy with life and a true kindness shimmers from our hearts. It shines forth and affects everyone around us.

The more I freed myself by looking deeply into my suffering and developed a relationship with these parts, I was able to embody and transmit kindness to others in small and large ways.

When I was honest with myself and I allowed each place to be known, I created more spaciousness in my body, mind, and spirit and was held in the arms of the Presence that doesn't come and go.

Becoming authentic and not living in a mold of how I thought I should be was liberating. Now I engage with simple acts of kindness from a truly open heart, which includes my difficulties, throughout the day.

32

FORGIVENESS

*"To everything there is a season, a time for every purpose
under the heaven. A time to be born and a time to die.
A time to plant and a time to harvest..."*

~Ecclesiastes 3:1-8

In October 2006, a man shot 11 children in a school in the Amish country in Pennsylvania. Five of the children died. There was an additional shock in that it happened in a community that is very insulated. It was the third deadly school shooting in the U.S. that week.

That afternoon, a grandfather of one of the girls who was murdered announced his forgiveness to the killer. Within days, most of that Amish community proclaimed their forgiveness to the killer and his family.

I was shocked and concerned by their pronouncements of forgiveness. Was it premature? And if so, how might that affect their healing process? Often, premature forgiveness can create more suffering.

That said, everybody grieves in their own time and in their own way. No two people will feel the same way about their experiences.

Forgiveness has been defined as the act of canceling a debt and freeing ourselves from bondage.

When we realize we aren't living fully and feel imprisoned in one way or another, we have the opportunity to begin the process of forgiveness.

Many psychotherapists, coaches, and healers think that forgiveness toward another needs to be expressed sooner than later and that it is necessary to do so whether the victim is ready or not. Other psychotherapists believe that the victim has to stop feeling anger or resentment, that the victim needs to let go, and that we have to forgive the perpetrator even when the person doesn't deserve forgiveness.

I whole-heartedly disagree!

This is what I've discovered through my personal healing process and being a psychotherapist and healer for more than 40 years.

Everyone struggles with forgiveness from all sorts of hurts.

It's not so easy to let go and heal from ruptured relationships and it's absurd to think that we need to forgive before we are ready.

The burdens we carry may be from our own conscious and/or unconscious misconduct along with the unprocessed trauma of our personal history and that of our ancestors. We carry the effects in our hearts, minds, bodies, and spirits. We often hold on to the emotions wrought from the infractions of others or the guilt from our own misguided actions.

Personally, I didn't want to manipulate myself by using forgiveness as a way to avoid suffering and think that I followed the path of right action. I knew that would be an escape from reality and recreate my survival defense of hiddenness. I also didn't want to be left with that terrible feeling of an internal negative void, that I just wasn't right and that I was fractured.

My commitment to myself was to honestly heal, transform, live as openly as I could and integrate into the totality and wholeness that was my truest nature, the person I was born to be.

I knew in my heart of hearts that something else needed to happen to truly experience authentic inner peace and a way to traverse the places that remained dystonic and troublesome.

Forgiveness was not on the menu until I allowed everything, or as much as I could tolerate at a time, to be touched and welcomed. I had to include my body and the shadowy parts of myself, too.

For many years, I worked with connecting the wounds I carried to my history, to my lineage, and my culture. I didn't leave anything out. I remembered and allowed what was once taboo and hidden to have a place in my heart.

As my heart opened, I grew a home for confusion, disgust, uncomfortable bodily sensations, fear, despair, resentment, sorrow, jealousy, competition, shame, murderous rage and probably more. I became more human, no longer terrified of my own shadow, and much more compassionate.

What was once hidden became palpable and alive. I was lighter, more present and real and I didn't have to hide anything from myself anymore. I slowly peeled away the layers of protection as my vital life force strengthened.

As I slowly developed a relationship with my suffering, the naturalness of forgiveness was gently cultivated.

Through honoring and accepting my limitations, my imperfections, my suffering, and my humanity, I opened my heart. There is a spaciousness that gives me breath, the ability to traverse dissonance without forcing anything. This gave birth to the natural rising of forgiveness that was always there and waiting for me to arrive.

Patience with my process, respecting my rhythm, self-forgiveness, and a deep commitment to truly living a life as a compassionate healing presence, created the key that unlocked my whole being.

This allowed a deeper, more complete, genuine forgiveness to grow that did not come from avoiding my suffering. Bit by bit, I reclaimed myself and of course I made mistakes along the way. It wasn't clear sailing. And I was able to support others in their healing journeys. Quite frankly if I had to do it again, I wouldn't change anything; well not much, anyway.

Today, I still carry hurt from a family member from childhood. I can't forgive her. And, I no longer judge myself for that.

Here's one of the practices I developed for myself:

I take a breath and hold the tension between me and this person close to my heart. I feel what's there, I allow the thoughts, I breathe. As I allow myself to be in touch with this tension, I feel my broken heart gently, usually for a few seconds.

Through this practice, I acknowledge myself and my suffering. I allow the various emotions to be touched, the thoughts to be heard, I bring them into my heart and breath even if it's just for a moment.

True forgiveness arises when I have truly allowed my resentment, hatred, vulnerability, loss, and grief to be acknowledged. It doesn't mean that I forget the past.

I no longer carry it apart from myself because I don't feel the need on any level to forgive her. And yet I don't want to have the inner fire of rage because of the lack of resolution with her; so I practice, awaken, heal, and pray.

This resets and transforms my body, my heart, my brain, my mind and my spirit — one moment at a time.

We want forgiveness to be a natural part of our healing into wholeness and our truest nature even when we experience difficulties with it.

Each time I enter this practice, which is quite often, I enter the beautiful field of forgiveness, which opens my heart a bit more; self-compassion flows in where it had been blocked before. What more can I ask for?

Self-forgiveness allows us to be liberated from the burdens and shackles of the past.

We don't have to carry the wounds of the past inside of us, we can forgive or be in the process of forgiveness after deeply being in relationship with the ruptures and wounds from various relationships.

When we directly experience the dissonance with the various people whom we have hurt and who have hurt us, there is more freedom and inner peace.

33

WHOLENESS

"You are already that which you seek."

-Ramana Maharshi

What if we are already the wholeness that we long for? And what is wholeness anyway?

On the spiritual level, wholeness is the fundamental underlying interconnectedness and interdependence of all of life.

On the personal, every day, human level, wholeness is the integration and embodiment of all the parts and aspects of who we are, mind-heart-body-spirit.

True wholeness includes the personal and the spiritual.

Wholeness has always been whispering to me; "come home, be all of who you are."

As a young girl, I often experienced wholeness as a nourishing presence in the wee hours of the morning. And simultaneously, throughout most of my childhood, adolescence, and young adulthood, I was aware of a deep sense of disconnection, loneliness, and separateness.

Clearly, I wasn't consciously in touch with the interconnectedness and interdependence of all things. I imagined that acquiring wholeness would save me from the hardships of life.

I was deluded.

For a long time, I searched for a personal and spiritual escape from my inner demons. I attempted to feel inner peace all the time. I believed that somehow, I would be more evolved, happier, and enlightened that way.

At some point I realized that the truth of impermanence and death were not my friends. Ironically, even though I feared death, I also feared being fully alive.

Fear had run my life! I'm not talking about the ordinary neurotic fear, I'm referring to the unconscious hum that had always been playing a soft, shrilling note. And inside that sound was the truth: "you will die."

The thought of dying was terrifying. So, it ran my life as an unconscious truth that prevented me from having what I deeply longed for—living an honest, real, and authentic life.

I couldn't tolerate the thought of death, anything but that! How could I possibly be seated in my wholeness? I couldn't.

I silenced and controlled it. I molded and exiled it. I sent it to the other end of the universe. Clearly, I didn't want to have anything to do with it. Why feel unsafe? I thought that just about anything was better than that.

I built obstacles that concealed my ability to be who I am. So, I stayed stuck and couldn't open into my greatness. Ugh!

Even though I wanted to be fully alive, the truth of death held me hostage. I was like the "walking dead." That was not how I wanted to live, yet it was how I had programmed myself to have a sense of safety.

But there was one problem, one huge problem: I wasn't really in life, well not fully, anyway. I was on the other side of a transparent divide, me here and everyone and everything else out there.

I erroneously thought that focusing on living well and the positives life had brought to me and cutting out the rest was the path to freedom, inner harmony, and soulfulness. But it was just the opposite.

I feared my own death and death in any form. And I split from reality by pushing my terror away. I thought that was a good thing until I realized it created more suffering.

When I woke up to all of this, I prayed to be authentic and live in the truth. I wanted an honest life filled with awareness that shimmered in the light of reality.

It was time to touch and heal my deepest suffering. That wouldn't happen until my friend's funeral.

We all gathered at a synagogue in Manhattan's Upper West Side. There were hundreds of people there. My heart was breaking for her young husband and toddler. She was the most beautiful, loving, and intelligent woman-mother-psychologist. She was diagnosed with cancer while she was pregnant, lived as a mother for a time, and a short while later she was gone.

Of course, I knew that terrible things happen to good people, but I didn't fully allow true suffering to penetrate my heart until then.

In that moment, my fear of ignoring the truth was stronger than my need to have a false sense of safety.

Allowing this truth to enter my being and break my heart changed me. It was a bit of a "mini-death." In fact, every time I change and assimilate more truths and realizations, I shift and experience a bit of a "mini-death." Simultaneously, the more I awaken to the reality of who I am and what the world is, I am freer and more open-hearted.

Without looking back, I jumped into a relationship with all of me and life as it is. I refused to exile any of the voices in my head or the sorrows in my heart—it hasn't been an easy path and yet I became more whole at each juncture.

My healing and awakening process wasn't linear. I traversed territories of joy and sorrow, shame and fierceness, rage and contentment, and tears and laughter. I touched the deepest parts of my woundedness.

When I omitted parts of the truth, I suffered more and was more separate from the wholeness that I longed for.

As I healed, I began to see myself and the world more clearly. It was not always easy to be in relationship with the truth and yet it was so freeing. I was willing to go beyond my personal beliefs and be shaken up.

I realized that I had manipulated myself to stay safe and protected and that I had limited my access to the full breath of life. Slowly, gently and with profound kindness, my heart opened, and I realized that I was already whole.

The seed of compassion began to blossom through my entire being and held me.

Layer by layer, I unveiled the unconscious wisdom that lived dormant inside of my heart.

I committed to practicing the art of "waking up" throughout the day. I could feel there was so much more to life than how I had lived, especially whenever I smelled the sweet perfume of wholeness.

For example, if I was saying something negative to myself—I might hear that voice and respond to it in a compassionate way whereas in the past I would curse it and summon it to be exiled. So now I say, "oh hi, I hear you and that's not true." or I laugh and say, "hi," acknowledging that voice in some compassionate way. It's pretty cool to experience it.

I refused to stop healing even when the times were messy and tough. I was absolutely devoted to finding ways to truly embody all of who I am. As I started to see things as they are, I was able to relax more. I didn't escape even when I wanted to.

Today, when I am triggered and emotionally activated, I feel it in my heart, I allow it, I listen to it and really work with it.

Last year was very difficult for our family. Our young grandson needed two surgeries. Even though I knew in my heart of hearts that he would survive the surgeries, I was anxious a lot of the time. I prayed, I engaged with various spiritual practices, and lots of healing.

By including all my fears, even the worst terror of the possibility of losing my dearest love, I was able to be present, gain stability, support him, and the family before, during and after the procedures.

I knew that I couldn't suffer alone. I reached out to my friends who were incredibly supportive. When people offered to pray for us, I wholeheartedly accepted.

My commitment to myself, my family, my clients, my students, and my friends, is to wake up and be liberated from the chains of history. As I saw who I truly was, past my historical wounds, I became more and more whole. My perception changed, I developed a clearer, wide-eyed lens into myself, others, and the world.

Sometimes, I still need to remind myself that all things are an expression of wholeness.

Realizing the truth about my impermanence, making room for the fact that everything changes, and nothing lasts forever, was the underlying foundation of consciousness that allowed me to heal, grow, and transform more than I ever imagined.

Wholeness calls and I answer.

34

WALKING THE PATH

"In the life of the spirit,
there is no ending that is not a beginning."

~Henrietta Szold

Experiencing the realization of wholeness was not the end of the path or a finishing; in many ways it was just the beginning. The path is more of a deepening and expanding spiral into all of reality that includes all of me, all of time, all of space, and even more than I know.

As I unwound the patterns of my history, as I rubbed the sleep out of my eyes, I gave each piece that was bound up in a trance a place in my heart.

Like in an alchemical experiment, as I held each piece closer than close, it was transmuted into its natural, original form. I discovered a true connection to all aspects of myself — my body, my emotions, my mind, and my spirit. I didn't leave anything out even when I wanted to.

My heart is constantly ripening. I have more room to breathe. I turn toward each moment in my imperfect way. Here now, now here ... being with each thing that rises.

I have a renewed appreciation for the small stuff. Watching my little grandson become thrilled in an instant when he sees a baby in the mirror brings delight to my heart.

As I have found my footing, I continue to dive deeper into life and reality. I still experience heartbreak and confusion, being open and being closed, joy and sorrow. My life is fuller, and I am freer.

Through the self-compassion I have cultivated, I remember that I am an imperfect woman who is committed to true liberation as I heal more and more of my self-critical, punishing, and judgmental self.

Traversing the fragile landscape of my vulnerability helps me to feel whole and touch the beauty of life.

As I continuously touch these tender places and vividly allow them to exist in me, I feel more compassion for all of us traversing this impermanent existence. It hasn't always been easy and yet there is manna in the desert.

I don't leave anything out even when I want to.

Feeling my grief when it is present is more healing and more of a blessing these days. Giving it a place in my heart helps me to feel present and to experience optimal vitality.

Realizing that there is wisdom in pain, adversity, dissonance, and resistance, I connect to my healing and awakening heart.

The first nondual healing that we teach in our school, *the Healing of Immanence*, awakened me to the profound depths of the illuminating truth — that there is divinity in every part of life and death.

Because of all of this, I am much more open to allowing each bud on the bush to flower at its pace and in its time. I never really know what will unfold as I allow the movement of life to be itself. I can't control it anyway. I tried that already, it is no longer my vocation.

When I am avoiding, contracting, distorting, and exiling I stop, breathe, and develop a relationship with it. I know there is something to learn.

Remembering my history, my lineage and my ancestors has shed light upon a profound gratitude. I can hear their prayers now. If they hadn't suffered and survived as they did, I wouldn't have this blessed life.

Every conversation I have is sacred, whether it is with one of my kitties, my husband, my son, my daughter in-law or my grandson, my friends, my students, and even an enemy here and there. Jamie and Josh used to make fun of me when I became friendly with someone who we met online at the movies or at an airport. I just love connecting with people, animals, and the beauty of the world. In those moments I am fully present and alive.

I allow myself to connect with life and things as they are.

I am deeply grateful to all the people in my life. I love our conversations and our exploration of life, whether it's about grief, family, food, reality, knitting, or creativity.

Oh, I love so many things in life, I can go on and on and have so many conversations. I am always reading books and exploring the world. There will never be enough time to read all the books I want to read. I remember that my father always had a stack of books next to his side of the bed. I get it now, there are so many books in my Kindle library and in the house. I read a few and recycle them and then I bring in too many more. Always loving the insights, learning something new, exploring how someone else did something similar to me or different from me, it's all so enlivening.

The beauty of art, a movie, a book, music, and just being where I am brings pleasure into the pores of my skin, fills me, and flows into my heart, opening it a bit more.

Allowing everything to be what it is and not run away. I am more here and real and centered.

Meditation and spiritual practices are part of my daily routine. I enter the field of healing and awakening each time I practice.

Remembering that I am imperfect, and life is imperfect, makes a difference; I feel freer. I don't have to grasp at a destination filled with self-improvement any longer. When I am triggered by something and get upset and have obsessive thoughts, I go inside with support and spend time with my heart so whatever the root of the disturbance is can be revealed and healed.

I need to remember that my healing work is not over. In fact, I have a feeling that there is always more to awaken to and to realize as long as I am here in this life and maybe even thereafter.

I have moments of uncertainty a lot of the time, I ride those ripples.

Intention helps me to set a goal that comes from my heart, my mind, and my soul. My deepest desire is to be a loving and healing presence filled with honesty and integrity — and to realize when I'm not.

My healing life path is all about love, compassion, gratitude, and giving everything, even the difficulties, a place in my heart.

35

GRATITUDE

"When eating fruit,
remember the one who planted the tree."

~Vietnamese Proverb

I am grateful, the palm trees are dancing, as they bend ever so gracefully, I am warmed by the wind.

The babbling of my grandson as he awakens from his nap, the kitties climbing on top of me saying good morning, the hand of my love as he touches me, my son tenderly holding his son.

When I sat down to write a few things I felt grateful for, in that moment, I experienced a radiating sensation coming from my heart. As I consciously took a breath, I settled into my body a bit more as my heart expanded throughout my whole chest.

As I continued to consciously breathe, the sensations touched and illuminated every part of me.

Gratitude rises in me when I experience an honest awareness of what I have in the moment. Sometimes it's in response to a gesture that someone makes toward me, or an interaction that I've had, sometimes it's from a simple awareness such as smelling a flower, or watching the birds eat their seed, or my kitty singing as I feed him. It can be from anything at all.

My experience with gratitude has been multi-faceted. Even though I have always felt grateful throughout my life, when I started to practice working with gratitude as a healing modality, I became acutely aware I had some internal emotional disconnections. I couldn't experience gratitude fully in my mind, my body, and my spirit.

Simultaneously, I was passionate about life and longed to be a fully present, open-hearted woman. So, I stepped into a direct inquiry with the disconnected place even though a part of me wanted to throw the baby out with the bathwater.

So instead of getting rid of her, I cared for her, I kept her close and allowed her to be what and whoever she was. As I held her close to my heart, we grew together. This took time and perseverance.

As I had so many times in the past, I climbed the ladder to the high diving board, I slowly inched to the end of the board, I closed my eyes, prayed, and jumped into the deep end of the pool.

My toes touched the bottom of the pool, with my knees bent, I pushed upward and instantaneously floated back to the surface for air. I was safe and scared. Why wasn't I living with an awareness that everything matters?

Having left myself out of the equation, I found my suffering and my joy in those healing waters. Sometimes it was ice cold as I was consumed with fear. Other times, it was warm and comforting.

As I included all of what emerged through inquiry, my heart opened, my edges softened, and I became much more vulnerable and real.

After a while, something new started to emerge. The more I held my discomforts, sorrow, anger, and fears close to my heart, I developed compassion toward myself. I was grateful to have reached that moment in my life.

Becoming more seated in my true self and wholehearted were the ingredients I needed to create a home in which true gratitude could live. I began to see that everything when held with respect and close enough can free us.

As my heart opened so did my brain. Recently, research has shown that as we work with gratitude, our brains release the "feel good" neurotransmitters, dopamine, and serotonin.

They have also discovered that it improves physical health and immunity against disease, that there is less reactivity from emotional triggers, more self-respect, and enhanced resilience.

Now, I am grateful for many things — even the simplest of things. I have gratitude for the chair I am sitting on. At this point in my life, I prefer to sit on furniture than sit on the floor. I even have gratitude toward the people who constructed the chair and the people who made the fabric that was used to make the chair comfortable. And I am grateful for the trees that grew the wood that was used for the construction of the chair.

There is a noise down the street that is annoying me. And, I have deep gratitude for it, as it helps me know that my hearing is functioning well enough. I became aware that I was annoyed and took the time to stop and breathe and open to the larger paradigm where gratitude lives.

So many experiences can be a portal into the awakening ground of gratitude if we have the heart to pause, breathe, and be with the moment.

GRATITUDE

Realizing my imperfection ... gratitude.
Remembering my loves ... gratitude.
Touching the earth ... gratitude.
Eating ... gratitude.
Drinking ... gratitude.
My home ... gratitude.
Trees ... gratitude.
Birds ... gratitude.
Sleeping ... gratitude.
Waking up... gratitude.
Healing ... gratitude.
Meditation ... gratitude.
Teaching ... gratitude.
Friends ... gratitude.
Clients ... gratitude.
Books ... gratitude.
Computers ... gratitude.
The sky ... gratitude.
Rain ... gratitude.
Snow ... gratitude.
Making love ... gratitude.
Animals ... gratitude.
Holiness ... gratitude.
Awareness ...gratitude.
Walking ... gratitude.
Crafting ... gratitude.
Art ... gratitude.
Music ... gratitude.
Guidance ... gratitude.
When I include all of myself and experience
the gift of life, I enter the portal of gratitude. It is good.
May we all be blessed.

36

IT'S ALL ABOUT LOVE

"And in the end,
the love you take is equal to the love you make."

~ The Beatles

*T*he *Torah*, more commonly known as *The Five Books of Moses*, is a sacred scripture that contains divine wisdom and revelation when a person is willing to directly contact the hidden sparks that lie within the stories. It conceals the mystery of this divine wisdom in the words and stories of our ancestors.

In Hebrew, every letter has a meaning, a numerical value and is what is referred to in Buddhism as "the thing itself." In other words, it doesn't symbolize anything. When you put these letters together in different ways, their meanings and their values change. The placement of the letters is significant.

The first word in the *Torah* is *bereshit* which means "in the beginning." The first letter of *bereshit* is a *bet* and it is the second letter of the Hebrew alphabet. *Bet* means duality, house, and creation. We need duality to house the world we live in, to allow creation to have a place to express its divine nature and to provide a focal point of holiness on Earth.

The last word of the *Torah* is *Yisrael*, "Israel," meaning all of you who wrestle with God and reality. The last letter of the word *Yisrael* is a *lamed* and has a numerical value of 30. *Lamed* means to teach, learn, study, or to instruct.

When the last letter of the *Torah*, *Lamed*, is combined with the first letter of the *Torah*, *Bet*, the word becomes *Lev* meaning heart, and the numerical number is 32. Other words with a value of 32 are strong, nothing, the life soul, feelings, affections, to conceal, volition, desire, and understanding.

The *Torah* is heart-filled with wisdom, revelation, uncertainty, war, peace, duality, and unity. It teaches us that a personal journey of learning and awakening must be encountered to develop the relationship with the heart that is healing.

Our awakening heart is kind and trustworthy. All our wrestling throughout our lives is a fundamental part of the creation itself.

This has sustained me.

Awakening my heart was the most natural thing to do; it clearly was my soul's longing. My path has been a journey filled with adventure, pitfalls, seemingly wrong turns, joy, and freedom. It has been the gradual discovery of returning home to my true nature.

Each day and within each moment, there is another opportunity for us to connect with the longing in our hearts and the abiding love that never comes and goes but is always present.

My intention, prayer, and commitment continue to carry me through the darkness. I remember and I forget, there is a lamp shining within the darkness.

My awakening heart allows me to love in a new way. Realizing that there is nowhere to go but here, I learned to pay attention to the natural unfolding of who I am moment to moment, breath after breath. I had to learn how not to get in the way of the natural streaming pulsation of life so that I could be present right where I am.

There have been many turning points in my life. These turnings points were the unique moments that profoundly influenced me. They were the moments when I stopped, breathed, turned toward myself, and said, "Here I am."

The writer, Anais Nin, said, "*And then the day came when the risk to remain tight in a bud was more painful than the risk it took to blossom.*" I decided to plunge into uncertainty and open to becoming a fully loving, compassionate, and imperfect human being. It took a deep commitment to myself to grow, open my heart and keep on keeping on.

Awakening my heart began when I started to listen to the longing in my heart; that small voice whispered, "Set me free, bring me home."

Once I committed to the risk that opened my heart and ushered me into the unknown, so much unfolded within me. Wrestling with the rusty gate that covered my heart, I became aware of the obstacles that I and life had placed before me.

I opened the gate and breathed.

My heart was hidden in a cave of grief. My awakening heart was sequestered deep inside and thirsty for the real. Everything was pulsating and glowing. I stepped in.

Uncovering the rubble of lifetimes, shedding layers, burning karma, metabolizing the life that is here, now.

Dark was the day. Dreams of heaven nourished me as I saw the eye that sees me. I always knew you were there, so close, and so far. Come closer.

In the highest places, inside the darkest caverns, traversing icy streams, I became the night sky to be with you.

Remembering that I am not alone.

Slowly and gently, I awakened as the ancient One whispered, "*The heart is the womb of creativity.*"

As my heart opened, layer by layer, I relaxed and descended into my truest self. I am who I was created to be. Love found me here; she is my sister and my brother.

The landscape I am a part of was revealed. I opened the gates, and as I entered, I realized that I belong. I am the landscape; the landscape is me.

There is One Heart, beating, healing, pulsating, breathing, and awakening. Receiving the nectar of the awakening Heart, I make love to the magnificent creation called life. Allowing a place in my heart for everything allows passion to flow through my being.

Here ... I Am home.

The true treasure is buried in the heart. Love is the one heart that holds this world together.

Fly a kite, paint the moon, climb a tree, roll down the hill, taste your snack, sing, shout, LIVE!

Be the love you already are.

ACKNOWLEDGMENTS

Writing this book has been quite the journey. It was hidden in my heart and soul for more than 30 years. There was always something else to work on.

I could not have completed this book without the support of these people.

Thank you, Jason Shulman, https://www.societyofsouls.com/, my spiritual teacher and dear friend, your introduction to this book completely melted my heart.

In 2019, Karen Hammond and Tasha Smith, https://emergesalestraining.com/, were teaching, coaching, and supporting me as I learned how to expand my essential oil business. One day I was talking with Karen and I told her how much I loved taking the time to create, write, and organize my social-media posts. Suddenly, there was a flash of inspiration that filled my mind, body, and spirit — I knew it was time to write my book. Thank you, Karen and Tasha.

So, I signed up for a Tom Bird, https://tombird.com/, virtual writing retreat. He held a great space for me; I was able to create, structure and write the first draft of my book in a weekend. I purchased his platinum program, knowing full well I needed to make an investment in my writing journey. Thank you, Tom.

Jeff Ellias-Frankel, my teaching partner, what can I say? Your heart and wisdom have been a source of comfort and inspiration for me for so many years. Thank you so much for your constant support while I took over 2 years to complete this book. And I am looking forward to making more music with you as we bring more healing and awakening into the world together. Thank you.

Without the ongoing support of Donna Velasco, my personal writing coach, I would have thrown my book project in the garbage a long time ago. Thank you, Donna.

Dani Antman, https://daniantman.com/, author of *Wired for God*, was always there cheering me on. We were able to commiserate about the ins and outs of writing a memoir. Thank you, Dani.

Neal, my dear brother, thank you for being the first person to read my manuscript and for letting me know what you were captured by and that you thought it was ready for editing.

Jane Sloven, https://www.janesloven.com/, also an author, was always, and I mean always, there for me when the going got tough. And, she made some great suggestions when she read my first draft of the manuscript. Thank you, Jane.

Denise Cassino, http://www.bestsellerservices.com/, has been a marketing extraordinaire and supportive genius for getting my book out there! She held my hand, she interpreted what seemed like a foreign language to me into a user friendly world. Thank you from the bottom of my heart.

Lucinda Rae, https://hellolucinda.com/, my goddess book cover designer, thank you for your desire to really "get" what I am trying to say to the world and transforming it into beauty.

Lila Edelkind, my dear knitting friend, thank you so much for reading and editing this book with a fine tooth comb, you helped me in ways that I didn't even know that I needed.

ACKNOWLEDGMENTS

Thank you to the wonderful women who helped me with my struggle to find the title: you confirmed my belief in the saying, "*It takes a village.*"

And to all my friends and family who have supported me on this book-writing journey, I would not have been able to complete it without your understanding and love. I often opted to stay home and write or to avoid writing. Trust me, I am looking forward to more playing, reading a few novels, more knitting, returning to my favorite museums and the theatre and moving back to my beloved Manhattan.

And thank you to all my clients and students who have danced on the spiraling paths of sorrow, joy, healing and awakening with me. Here's the book that so many of you have asked for over the years.

With so many blessings and much love.

REFERENCES

All the listed articles,
poems and books have deeply influenced me.

Antisemitism:

Night: Elie Wisel, Hill & Wang; 1960.

Antisemitism: Here and Now: Deborah E. Lipstadt, Schocken Books, 2019.

It Could Happen Here: Why America is Tipping from Hate to the Unthinkable—And How We Can Stop It, Jonathan Greenblatt, Mariner Books, 2022.

The Jews Should Keep Quiet: Franklin D. Roosevelt, Rabbi Stephen S. Wise, and the Holocaust: Rafael Medoff, Jewish Publication Society, 2021.

Birth Trauma:

12 Things Moms Did In The '50s That Not a Single Mom Would Do Today: https://www.romper.com/p/12-things-moms-did-in-the-50s-that-not-a-single-mom-would-do-today-24688

American Obstetrics in the 1950s: https://evidencebased-birth.com/american-obstetrics-in-the-1950s/.

Forceps Birth Delivery and Complications from the Birth Injury Help Center: https://www.birthinjuryhelpcenter.org/forceps-birth-in-jury.html.

Are Forceps Outdated?: https://www.angellawpc.com/blog/2020/february/are-forceps-outdated-/.

Obstetrical Forceps: https://enwikipedia.org/wiki/Obstetrical_forceps.

The Embryo Project Encyclopedia: Twilight Sleep: https://embryo.asu.edu/pages/twilight-sleep#:~:text=Twilight%20Sleep%20(Dammerschlaf)%20was%20a,no%20recollection%20of%20the%20procedure

Buddhism:

Mother of the Buddhas, Meditations on the Prajnaparamita Sutra, Lex Hixon, Quest Books 1993.

Treasury of the True Dharma Eye: Zen Master Dogen's Shobo Genzo, Kazuaki Tanahashi (editor), 2013.

Essential Oils:

my.doterra.com/eileensoils

Forgiveness:

Amish School Shooting: https://en.wikipedia.org/wiki/West_
Nickel_Mines_School_shooting, 2006.

*The Courage to Heal – Fourth Edition - Revised and Expanded:
A Guide for Women Survivors of Child Sexual Abuse*, Ellen
Bass, Laura Davis, Harper Paperbacks, 2008.

Gestalt Therapy:

Ego, hunger and aggression: The beginning of gestalt therapy,
F. S. Perls, 1969.

Living at the Boundary, Laura Perls, A Gestalt Journal
Publication, 1992.

*Gestalt Therapy: EXCITEMENT AND GROWTH IN
THE HUMAN PERSONALITY*, Frederick S. Perls, Ralph
Hefferline & Paul Goodman, 1951.

Guru Abuse:

Sexual Abuse by Yoga Gurus: https://en.wikipedia.org/wiki/
Sexual_abuse_by_yoga_ gurus#.

Kabbalah:

Kabbalistic Healing: A Path to an Awakened Soul: Jason
Shulman, Inner Traditions, 2004.

The Thirteen Petalled Rose: Adin Steinsaltz, Koren Publishers
Jerusalem, 2010.

Kabbalah: Gershon Scholem, Doreset Press, 1987.

Pirkei Avot: Wisdom of the Jewish Sages, Ktav Publishing, 1997.

Zohar: Pritzker Edition: Volumes 1-4, Daniel C. Matt (editor, translator), 2004-2007.

Kindness:

Conscience and Courage: Rescuers of Jews during the Holocaust, Eva Fogelman, Anchor, 1995.

Anne Frank Remembered: The Story of the Woman Who Helped to Hide the Frank Family, Miep Gies, Alison Leslie Gold, Simon & Schuster, 2009.

Nondual Healing:

Beyond The Now: Essays On The Heart Of Enlightenment, Jason Shulman, 2021.

RE-BREATHING BUDDHA'S FOUR NOBLE TRUTHS, *Jason Shulman* 2019.

THE NONDUAL SHAMAN: A CONTEMPORARY SHAMANISTIC PATH & THOROUGHGOING TRAINING FOR AWAKENING THE SELF, Jason Shulman, 2018.

The Instruction Manual For Receiving God, Jason Shulman, Sounds True, 2006.

THE NONDUAL PROCESS FOR CONFLICT RESO-LUTION, A Revolutionary Process for Resolving Conflict in Ourselves and Our World, Jason Shulman, 2022.

Rainforest:

https://www.thoughtco.com/tropical-rainforests-natures-medicine-cabinet-1204030

Transgenerational Trauma:

https://en.wikipedia.org/wiki/Transgenerational_epigenetic_inheritance#:~:text=Transgeerational%20epigenetic%20

inheritance%20is%20the,%E2%80%94in%20other%20words%2C%20epigenetically.

Inherited Trauma Shapes Your Health, Olga Kazan:

https://www.theatlantic.com/health/archive/2018/10/trauma-inherited-generations/573055/.

Jewish Trauma May Be Passed Down Through The Generations, Gila Lyons: https://www.harleytherapy.co.uk/counselling/what-is-transgenerational-trauma.htm.

https://medium.com/the-establishment/for-jewish-people-trauma-is-passed-down-across-generations-bf9aa503778b.

The Neurobiology of Transgenerational Trauma, Dr. Arielle Schwartz: https://drarielleschwartz.com/the-neurobiology-of-transgenerational-trauma-dr-arielle-schwartz/#.YzNMM-zMLow.

Do Jews Carry Trauma in Our Genes? A Conversation with Rachel Yehuda:
https://www.tabletmag.com/sections/arts-letters/articles/trauma-genes-q-a-rachel-yehuda

Learning from epigenetics: learning from ancestral wisdom and science:
https://www.swanaancestralhub.org/home/learning-from-epigenetics-linking-ancestral-wisdom-and-science.

How Trauma and Resilience Cross Generations:
https://onbeing.org/programs/rachel-yehuda-how-trauma-and-resilience-cross-generations-nov2017/.

How Does Intergenerational Trauma Work?
https://www.verywellhealth.com/intergenerational-trauma-5191638.

Intergenerational transmission of trauma effects: putative role of epigenetic mechanisms:
https://www.ncbi.nlm.nih.gov/pmc/articles/PMC6127768/.

Transgenerational transmission of trauma and resilience: A qualitative study with Brazilian offspring of Holocaust survivors:
https://www.ncbi.nlm.nih.gov/pmc/articles/PMC3500267/.

DNA can carry memories of traumatic stress down the generations:
https://cordis.europa.eu/article/id/122740-dna-can-carry-memories-of-traumatic-stress-down-the-generations.

Intergenerational transmission of paternal trauma among US Civil War ex-POWs:
https://www.pnas.org/doi/10.1073/pnas.1803630115.

REFERENCES

Torah:

The Living Torah: The Five Books of Moses and the Haftarah: (Hebrew and English edition), Rabbi Aryeh Kaplan, Mozanim, 1981.

Quotes:

Mary Oliver: *Summer Day, Devotion: The Selected Poems of Mary Oliver*, 2020.

Barbara Kingsolver: *The Bean Trees: The Strength of Motherhood,* Harper Torch, 2013.

Naomi Shihab Nye: *Kindness,* Words Under the Words: Selected Poems, The Eighth Mountain Press, 1994.

Rainer Maria Rilke: *Letters to a Young Poet,* 1929.

Larry Dossey: *Prayer Is Good Medicine: How to Reap the Benefits of Prayer*, Harper San Francisco, 1996.

Anatole France: *The Petit Pierre, French Edition,* 1918. Viktor E. Frankl: *Man's Search For Meaning*, Beacon Press, 2006. (newer editions available)

Jack Kerouac: *On The Road*, Viking Press, 1957.

Albert Einstein: *Saturday Evening Post* interview, 1929.

Barbara Myerhoff: https://en.wikipedia.org/wiki/Barbara_ Myerhoff.

Carl G. Jung: *Synchronicity: An Acausal Connecting Principle*, R. F. C. Hull (translator), Princeton University Press, 2010.

Kazu Haga: Founder, East Point Academy, https://www.middlebury.edu/institute/people/kazu-haga.

Dogen Zenji: *Master Dogen's Shobogenzo, Book 1*, 2006.

Shekhar Kapur: filmmaker: https://shekharkapur.com/blog/.

Thich Nhat Hahn, https://uplift.love/thich-nhat-hanh-awakening-from-the-illusion-of-separation.

Sunryo Suzuki: *Zen Mind, Beginner's Mind*, Weatherhill, 1970.

Elizabeth Holzman: https://en.wikipedia.org/wiki/Elizabeth_Holtzman.

Antoine de Saint-Exupery: *The Little Prince*, Richard Howard (translator), 2000.

Bernie Siegel MD: *Love, Medicine and Miracles*, Harper and Row, 1986.

Chris Williamson: *Song of the Soul*, from *Circle of Friends*, 1991.

Jhumpa Lahiri: *In Other Words*, Vintage, 2017.

John Lennon: *Power To The People*, Ono Plastic Band, 1971.

Rumi: *A Year With Rumi: Daily Readings*, translated by Coleman Barks, 2006.

REFERENCES

Buckminster Fuller: *The American Scholar*: Planetary Planning, 1970.

Amelia Earheart: https://en.wikipedia.org/wiki/Amelia_ Earhart.

Anatole France: *The Petite Pierre*, G. P. Ballin (editor), Create Space Independent, 2014.

Ramana Maharshi: *Be As You Are: The Teachings Of Ramana Maharshi*, edited by David Godman, Penguin UK, 1988.

Henrietta Szold: https://en.wikipedia.org/wiki/Henrietta_ Szold.

The Beatles: *The End*, *Abbey Road*: Apple Records.

ABOUT THE AUTHOR

Eileen Marder-Mirman's pas-
sion is to help people to be free.
Throughout her entire life, having
the normal experiences of grief,
loss, and celebration, she has always
stayed aligned with knowing she is
part of a larger reality and is committed to help others feel guided,
and on the path to healing and
authenticity.

As a New York State Licensed Mental Health Counselor
and a spiritual healing teacher for more than 45 years,
Eileen specializes in integrating psychotherapy, spirituality,
meditation, and various forms of alternative healing in her
private practice. For the past 20 years, she has been a senior
teacher and supervisor at A Society of Souls, The School for
Nondual Healing and Awakening.

Eileen has led numerous healing retreats in Europe and
the United States and has practiced meditation for 50 years.
She graduated from Syracuse University with a Master's in
Counseling in 1977 and continuously studies new psycho-
logical and healing modalities such as Nondual Kabbalistic
Healing, Gestalt Therapy, PSYCH-K®, energy psychology,

Therapeutic Touch, Reiki, and the therapeutic use of aromatherapy.

Eileen believes that it's never too late to wake up to becoming the authentic person you were born to be. And most importantly, we don't have to stay stuck in the patterns of our history!

Eileen lives in New York with her husband and two cats and makes sure that she sees her grandson every week. When she isn't healing or teaching, she is knitting, exploring art and going to the theater in New York (again and again). You might also find her obsessing over new apartments or recovering from colds she gets from her grandson's daycare. Her greatest joy in life is her family both near and far.

RESOURCES

Stop The B***S*** Healing Classes

From time to time, we get a group together to walk through the process of healing our b***s***. We have an introductory workshop to start on this journey together, and a 6-week program where we will explore our definition of "freedom," our beliefs, and simple actions we can take to lead to more fulfillment in life.

Don't worry, there won't be any meditation.

To learn more, go to https://www.eileenmardermirman.com/

Virtual Speaking Events/Podcast Interviews

Eileen is available for virtual speaking events and podcast interviews. Eileen's work focuses on healing practices for middle-aged professional women who are open to walking in their spiritual journey with others.

Email for more information, healerma@gmail.com.

Aromatherapy & Essential Oils To Support Healing

Eileen would be happy to assist you and your family on your healing journey by advising you on therapeutic grade essential oils that would align with what you need more.

Email for more information, healerma@gmail.com

Connect with Eileen

WEBSITE: https://www.eileenmardermirman.com/

INSTAGRAM: @eileenmardermirman

FACEBOOK: https://www.facebook.com/eileen.mardermirman

LINKED IN: https://www.linkedin.com/in/eileen-marder-mirman-206a4530/

TWITTER: @healermama

Made in United States
Orlando, FL
05 April 2023

31793257R00146